DISCARD

Philip Pullman

WHO
WROTE
THAT?

Philip Pullman

Margaret Speaker Yuan

Foreword by
Kyle Zimmer

CHELSEA HOUSE
PUBLISHERS
A Haights Cross Communications Company ®
Philadelphia

CHELSEA HOUSE PUBLISHERS

VP, NEW PRODUCT DEVELOPMENT Sally Cheney
DIRECTOR OF PRODUCTION Kim Shinners
CREATIVE MANAGER Takeshi Takahashi
MANUFACTURING MANAGER Diann Grasse

STAFF FOR PHILIP PULLMAN

EXECUTIVE EDITOR Matt Uhler
EDITORIAL ASSISTANT Sarah Sharpless
PRODUCTION EDITOR Noelle Nardone
PHOTO EDITOR Sarah Bloom
INTERIOR AND COVER DESIGNER Keith Trego
LAYOUT 21st Century Publishing and Communications, Inc.

http://www.chelseahouse.com

A Haights Cross Communications ✦ Company ®

First Printing

1 3 5 7 9 8 6 4 2

Library of Congress Cataloging-in-Publication Data

Speaker-Yuan, Margaret.
   Philip Pullman/Margaret Speaker Yuan
      p. cm.—(Who wrote that?)
   Includes bibliographical references and index.
   ISBN 0-7910-8658-5
   1. Pullman, Philip, 1946– Juvenile literature. 2. Authors, English—20th century—
Biography—Juvenile literature. 3. Young adult fiction—Authorship—Juvenile
literature. 4. Fantasy fiction—Authorship—Juvenile literature. I. Title. II. Series.
PR6066.U44Z87 2005
823'.916—dc22
                                                                    2005008184

Table of Contents

FOREWORD BY
KYLE ZIMMER
PRESIDENT, FIRST BOOK

HUMANITY IS POWERED by stories. From our earliest days as thinking beings, we employed every available tool to tell each other stories. We danced, drew pictures on the walls of our caves, spoke, and sang. All of this extraordinary effort was designed to entertain, recount the news of the day, explain natural occurrences—and then gradually to build religious and cultural traditions and establish the common bonds and continuity that eventually formed civilizations. Stories are the most powerful force in the universe; they are the primary element that has distinguished our evolutionary path.

Our love of the story has not diminished with time. Enormous segments of societies are devoted to the art of storytelling. Book sales in the United States alone topped $26 billion last year; movie studios spend fortunes to create and promote stories; and the news industry is more pervasive in its presence than ever before.

There is no mystery to our fascination. Great stories are magic. They can introduce us to new cultures, or remind us of the nobility and failures of our own, inspire us to greatness or scare us to death; but above all, stories provide human insight on a level that is unavailable through any other source. In fact, stories connect each of us to the rest of humanity not just in our own time, but also throughout history.

This special magic of books is the greatest treasure that we can hand down from generation to generation. In fact, that spark in a child that comes from books became the motivation for the creation of my organization, First Book, a national literacy program with a simple mission: to provide new books to the most disadvantaged children. At present, First Book has been at work in hundreds of communities for over a decade. Every year children in need receive millions of books through our organization and millions more are provided through dedicated literacy institutions across the United States and around the world. In addition, groups of people dedicate themselves tirelessly to working with children to share reading and stories in every imaginable setting from schools to the streets. Of course, this Herculean effort serves many important goals. Literacy translates to productivity and employability in life and many other valid and even essential elements. But at the heart of this movement are people who love stories, love to read, and want desperately to ensure that no one misses the wonderful possibilities that reading provides.

When thinking about the importance of books, there is an overwhelming urge to cite the literary devotion of great minds. Some have written of the magnitude of the importance of literature. Amy Lowell, an American poet, captured the concept when she said, "Books are more than books. They are the life, the very heart and core of ages past, the reason why men lived and worked and died, the essence and quintessence of their lives." Others have spoken of their personal obsession with books, as in Thomas Jefferson's simple statement, "I live for books." But more compelling, perhaps, is the almost instinctive excitement in children for books and stories.

Throughout my years at First Book, I have heard truly extraordinary stories about the power of books in the lives of children. In one case, a homeless child, who had been bounced from one location to another, later resurfaced—and the only possession that he had fought to keep was the book he was given as part of a First Book distribution months earlier. More recently, I met a child who, upon receiving the book he wanted, flashed a big smile and said, "This is my big chance!" These snapshots reveal the true power of books and stories to give hope and change lives.

As these children grow up and continue to develop their love of reading, they will owe a profound debt to those volunteers who reached out to them—a debt that they may repay by reaching out to spark the next generation of readers. But there is a greater debt owed by all of us—a debt to the storytellers, the authors, who have bound us together, inspired our leaders, fueled our civilizations, and helped us put our children to sleep with their heads full of images and ideas.

WHO WROTE THAT? is a series of books dedicated to introducing us to a few of these incredible individuals. While we have almost always honored stories, we have not uniformly honored storytellers. In fact, some of the most important authors have toiled in complete obscurity throughout their lives or have been openly persecuted for the uncomfortable truths that they have laid before us. When confronted with the magnitude of their written work or perhaps the daily grind of our own, we can forget that writers are people. They struggle through the same daily indignities and dental appointments, and they experience the intense joy and bottomless despair that many of us do. Yet somehow they rise above it all to deliver a powerful thread that connects us all. It is a rare honor to have the opportunity that these books provide to share the lives of these extraordinary people. Enjoy.

As a boy, Philip Pullman lived in Australia for two years. Australia's unique wildlife, like the kangaroo pictured here, and its nighttime constellations—quite different in Pullman's new-found southern hemisphere home—held great fascination for the budding storyteller. It was here in Australia that Pullman fell in love with comic books and their tales of daring superheros. His favorite was Batman. The experience of living in Australia no doubt inspired the storyteller in Pullman, and he often created fantastic tales to entertain his younger brother, Francis.

1

A Childhood Full of Stories

TWO SMALL BOYS, brothers Philip and Francis Pullman, lay under the covers in the bedroom that they shared. With the lights out, Philip Pullman began to tell a story to his younger brother. Pullman made up the story as he went along. He wondered how the story would "come out" as he put it. He never knew, when he began to speak, whether or not he would be able to make sense of the story, or if it would come to a neat ending. In a short autobiographical sketch, Pullman wrote:

I remember the exhilaration of the risk: Would I find something to say? Would I dry up? And I remember the thrill, the bliss, when, a minute ahead of getting there, I saw a twist I could give to the end, a clever way of bringing back that character who'd come into it earlier and vanished inconclusively, a neat phrase to tie it all up with.[1]

The brothers had recently moved to Adelaide, Australia, with their mother and stepfather. In Australia, they found that there were many fascinating new sights. The southern sky contained new constellations. The wildlife was made up of different animals than the ones the boys had been accustomed to seeing in England. There was, however, outside of nature walks, very little entertainment for children. Television was not available in Australia in the early 1960s. An important part of the boys' life in Australia became the radio. Pullman's favorite radio program was "Superman." The announcer always began the show with the words, "Faster than a speeding bullet! More powerful than a locomotive! Able to leap tall buildings with a single bound! Look! Up there in the sky! Is it a bird? Is it a plane? No, it's Superman!"[2]

When Pullman had lived in England, Superman comic books were not available at the time. The authorities banned many comic books, as it was believed they were too violent and too full of lurid drawings to be appropriate for children. Comic books that were banned included stories of Batman, Captain America, Dick Tracy, and Superman. When the family moved to Australia, Pullman's stepfather bought him his first superhero comic books. Pullman particularly loved Batman. He pored over the "poorly printed stories on their cheap yellowing newsprint."[3] What he liked most was to dream about the world of Batman. He wanted to weave stories set in the glamorous streets of Gotham City, with spectacular villains, great dialogue, and fantastic pictures. He didn't want to be Batman, but Pullman wanted to write about him. He wrote, "I wanted to brood over the world of Batman, and dream actively . . . It was the first stirring of the story-telling impulse . . . I knew, instinctively, at once, that the telling of stories was delicious."[4]

Pullman's discovery of the power of telling tales, during his family's two-year stay in Australia, was the beginning of a lifelong fascination with storytelling. As Pullman later wrote, "Stories are the most important thing in the world. Without stories, we wouldn't be human at all."[5]

Philip Pullman was born on October 19, 1946, in Norwich, England. His father, Alfred Pullman, was a Royal Air Force (RAF) pilot. As was common in the 1940s, Pullman's mother, Audrey Pullman, did not work. Instead she stayed home to raise her son. Soon a second son, Francis, was born. When Pullman was six, his father was posted to Southern Rhodesia (now Zimbabwe), a southern African country and former British colony.

In Rhodesia, people were segregated by their skin color. There were strict controls on how Africans were allowed to mingle with white people. Africans had limited political and economic rights. The majority of land was owned by white people, while Africans were employed as laborers or servants.

As part of the British Empire, Rhodesia was a self-governing colony. It had its own legislature, civil service, armed forces, and police. Rhodesia was never administered directly from London. However, the British government had the right to intervene in the affairs of the colony. When Africans who wanted greater political rights rebelled, Britain provided members of its army and air force to fight on behalf of the colonial government.

Pullman as a 6-year-old boy was not conscious of the political realities concerning the colonial system. He wrote, "[I had] absolutely no idea about politics. I had friends of both races but I was dimly aware that there was a difference, and that black people were poorer than white people. I had no idea why."[6]

The conflict in Rhodesia had an enormous impact on Pullman's future. The rebellion against colonial rule brought his family to Africa. Many people in England hoped that negotiations would lead to an end of the conflict. They feared that chaos and a bloodbath would occur if colonial rule were overthrown by violence. As an RAF pilot, Alfred was sent to Africa to help end the rebellion and to help restore peace.

When Pullman's family left England, they traveled by ocean liner to Africa. Most international travel in the 1950s

Did you know...

Philip Pullman and his family went through the Suez Canal on their voyage from England to Australia. The Suez Canal extended from Port Said to Port Tawfiq (near Suez), connecting the Mediterranean Sea with the Red Sea. The canal was about 100 miles long.

The canal was planned by the French engineer Ferdinand de Lesseps, who also supervised its construction (1859–1869). The Convention of Constantinople was signed in 1888 by all major European powers of the time. It declared the canal neutral and guaranteed free passage to ships of all nations in both peace and wartime. Egyptian President Gamal Abdel Nasser nationalized the Suez Canal in July 1956. When Pullman transited the canal, it was still operated by the British.

was by sea rather than by air—air travel was just beginning to be developed. Planes did not have jet engines yet; instead, they had propeller-driven engines. The first jet airliner, the Boeing 707, was introduced in 1959. Throughout the 1950s and well into the 1960s, voyages by sea were more common than air travel.

Pullman was too young to remember much about the ocean voyage that took him to Africa, but he has vivid memories of Africa itself. He went to a new school, where the uniform included a kind of soft felt hat called a trilby. There was a story that a ghost haunted the school. Another ghost was said to live in a little electrical substation, a concrete building that gave out a constant electrical hum. The story was that an African had gone inside the building, despite the danger sign on the door, and had been electrocuted. His spirit remained in the building. Pullman wrote that the hum of electricity has had a ghostly quality for him ever since.

There were other interesting sights in Africa. Audrey acted in plays at a local amateur theater. Seeing her tears one morning on the stage, Pullman did not understand that she was acting. He wanted to comfort her. He was told that it was only a rehearsal for a play.

Some evenings, Alfred took his sons to see boxing matches in the compound, an area where the Africans lived. At other times, the smell of roasting ears of corn, called mealies, drifted over from the compound to the area where the white people lived. Pullman loved the smell of mealies. Years later, when he smelled the same aroma in a street market in London, Pullman felt tears come to his eyes at the reminder of his time in Africa.

As the political violence in Rhodesia escalated, Pullman returned to England with his mother and Francis. In Africa, Alfred flew combat missions against the revolutionaries, called the Mau Mau. He risked his life in the conflict, often flying over the border into Kenya, where the Mau Mau insurgency was the strongest.

Pullman was happy to return to England, because his family was able to stay with his mother's parents. Pullman's grandfather, Reverend Merrifield, was a clergyman, the rector of a village called Drayton in the county of Norfolk, on the east coast of England. Eight-year-old Pullman was eager to taste his grandmother's cooking again. He wrote, "One thing they didn't have in Africa was fried bread. Granny used to make fried bread, and I missed it."[7]

Pullman's grandparents lived in the rectory with his grandmother's sister. The rectory was a large house provided by the parish and it was always busy. People called constantly on Pullman's grandfather for spiritual guidance. As a parish priest, he was responsible for the daily worship services. He also officiated at weddings, christenings, and funerals. Pullman remembered his grandfather in his cassock (a close-fitting ankle-length garment worn by the clergy) and white surplice (a loose, knee-length white outer church garment with large open sleeves), as being "the centre of the world. There was no one stronger than he was, or wiser, or kinder. When I was young, he was the sun at the centre of my life. He told stories . . ."[8]

One story that Reverend Merrifield told was that of his friend Fred Austin. He and Austin had served in France during World War I. When Fred returned home after the war, the infant daughter he had left behind had grown into a little girl who did not recognize him. She ran away from him, afraid of the strange man with large hands and a loud laugh. With patience and kindness, Fred coaxed her until she trusted him and would come to him willingly. Pullman wrote, "When Grandpa told that story he said that God would appear to us like that; at first we'd be alarmed and frightened by him, but eventually we'd come to trust in his love." Later in life, Pullman found a similar story in the *Iliad*, the ancient Greek epic poem about the war between the Greeks and the Trojans. Hector, the prince of Troy, found his son playing on the battlements of the city. Not recognizing his father because of the plumed helmet the prince wore, the boy ran away into the arms of his nurse. When Hector removed his war helmet, the boy saw his father's face and was reassured. Pullman wrote, "Between my childhood and now, I've lost sight of God; but Hector the Trojan prince and Fred Austin the Devonshire soldier are still brightly alive to me; and so is Grandpa."[9]

Tragic news came in the form of a telegram from Africa when the family was staying in Drayton. Lieutenant Pullman had been shot and killed by the revolutionary Mau Mau forces while he flew a mission over Kenya. When their grandmother told them the news, Pullman and Francis were not able to understand what had happened, nor were they able to comprehend what it meant for their future. They had not seen their father for a long time, and he had been a distant figure even when they had all lived together in Africa. Pullman remembers that he did not really feel sad at the time because of these reasons. Soon after they were told the news, the brothers went back to playing outside in the garden.

The death of their father caused many changes in the children's lives. They remained with their grandparents in Drayton while Audrey went to work for the British Broadcasting Service in London. When the boys went to visit her, they saw a life that seemed very glamorous. Their mother lived in a flat in Chelsea. Pullman wrote, "She had lots of friends, and they were all young and pretty or handsome; the women wore hats and gloves to go to work, their dresses were long and flowery, and the men drove sports cars and smoked pipes, and there was always laughter, and the sun shone every day." [10]

On one visit, the boys and their mother were invited by Queen Elizabeth to a ceremony at Buckingham Palace—the queen's residence in London. Pullman and Francis wore gray suits with short trousers. Audrey wore a black dress because she was a widow. The family was met by a uniformed man who instructed the boys how to bow when the queen entered the room. He told them to address her as "Ma'am." When she left the room, they were supposed to bow again.

When Queen Elizabeth arrived, the boys performed their bows as they had been taught. The queen gave Audrey a medal in a blue case. It was a Distinguished Flying Cross (DFC), awarded after his death to Lieutenant Alfred Pullman. The ceremony, called an investiture, was private. The medal was the first DFC awarded during the conflict in Kenya. After the ceremony, outside the palace, photographs were taken of the boys and their mother. One of the photographs was printed in the local paper, the *Eastern Evening News*, with an article about Pullman's father.

Later in life, when Pullman learned more about his parents, he wrote:

> One curious thing about growing up is that you don't only move forward in time; you move backwards as well, as pieces of your parents' and grandparents' lives come to you. And it was only when I was a grown man that I found about more of the truth about my father, and I don't suppose I shall ever know the whole of it. Apparently he had been in all kinds of trouble . . . he had had to agree to a separation from my mother . . . So all of my life I've had the idea that my father was a hero cut down in his prime, a warrior, a man of shining glamour, and none of it was

Philip Pullman, pictured here, has become a best-selling author on book lists for both children and adults. His books include **The Shadow in the North,** **The Golden Compass,** *and* **The Amber Spyglass.**

true. Sometimes I think he's really alive somewhere in hiding, with a different name. I'd love to meet him.[11]

After a year of mourning, Pullman's mother remarried. Her new husband was an RAF pilot whom they had known in Africa as Uncle Johnny. Soon there was another change. The family was off to Australia, where the RAF had transferred Johnny, the boys' new stepfather.

The trip to Australia was again by boat. The liner went from England down the Atlantic coasts of Portugal and Spain. It passed the Straits of Gibraltar into the Mediterranean, then sailed to Egypt. The ship sailed through the Suez Canal into the Indian Ocean. There were stops in India before the ship crossed the Indian Ocean to Australia. The voyage took several weeks. About the trip, Pullman wrote:

I remember a lot about the voyage to Australia . . . how grateful I am to have lived at a time when, if you made a long journey, you traveled on the surface of the earth. One thing we've lost with air travel is a sense of how large the world is, and how various. Five miles up in a jumbo jet, what can you see? The in-flight movie, that's what you can see. But aboard ship, the world was close, and all our senses knew it.[12]

For example, the senses of taste and smell and hearing were heightened. As was common with most cruises in those days, there were five meals a day. In the morning there was breakfast and elevenses (bouillon or ice cream, depending on the weather). Then there was lunch, followed by after-noon tea. Tea featured trolleys of cakes, pastries, and dainty triangular sandwiches. A piano played tunes from popular musicals of the day. Later there was dinner. At dinner, dress was formal. The men wore dinner jackets and the ladies wore evening gowns. After dinner, there was dancing and other entertainment. Many people played bridge. There was the late-night supper, and snacks were provided between meals if anyone had an urge for them. The dance band played until late in the evening. The lounge smelled of cocktails, cigarettes, and elegant perfumes.

Nothing, however, was quite as spectacular as the ocean.

So many different colors! So many different kinds of waves! And the different ways they made the ship move. Rolling from side to side was all right; you got used to that. But when the bow rose high and then plunged down sickeningly only to groan and rise again towards the next inevitable plunge, you stopped thinking of food and glamour and wanted to die. Then there were days and nights when the sea was as flat as a map, when the sun glared and the stars blazed.[13]

Life at sea, however, was not all dining, listening to music, watching the ocean, or even getting seasick. Francis and Pullman both came down with scarlet fever. They had to stay in their cabins. There were few choices in activities for the boys while they were sick. In the 1950s there were no computers, no video games, and no DVDs. To amuse themselves, the boys had books, board games like checkers or chess, and fantasy games that they invented. They had a construction set that they used to build forts and castles. They fought imaginary battles that lasted days at a time. The boys frequently changed roles from being good guys to being bad guys. Their games led the way for the stories that Pullman began to tell during their stay in Australia.

By the time they reached the equator, Pullman and Francis were well enough to enjoy "crossing the line" from the Northern to the Southern Hemisphere. Crossing the line was an old-time ceremony where King Neptune came aboard with his court. He set up his throne in the swimming pool. Anyone who had never crossed the equator before had to be dunked in the pool as a tribute to Neptune. Although both boys had already crossed the line on their trip to Africa, they were allowed to join in the fun again. They were given certificates that promised King Neptune's help should they ever need it.

Eight-year-old Pullman met and fell in love with a young girl on the voyage to Australia. She was dark-haired and pretty, and her name was Geraldine. Pullman desperately wanted to kiss her. Somewhere in the Indian Ocean, his wish came true. "And I vividly remember thinking as I kissed her in that half-darkened cabin how lucky I was, that I had only to think of a thing and it would happen; and that sense of being blessed by fortune has never entirely left me." [14]

While growing up, Philip Pullman found that poetry was a substantial source of inspiration for a budding writer. He read a lot of poetry in school, including works by the English poets John Milton (1608–1674) (pictured here), William Wordsworth (1770–1850), and William Blake (1757–1827). Milton's language, in particular, captured his imagination.

2

Village Life

THE FAMILY REMAINED in Australia for almost two years. When they returned to England, they lived briefly in London before moving again, this time to a village called Llanbedr in Gwynedd county, Wales. Wales is one of the countries that makes up the United Kingdom, along with Northern Ireland, Scotland, and England. Located far to the west of London, Llanbedr, was a small, rural village situated on the coast of the Irish Sea. The family moved into a house in the woods about a half-mile from the village. Known for its physical beauty and superb beaches, Llanbedr was Pullman's home for 10 years. It was the longest period of time that he stayed in one place during his childhood.

Pullman's stepfather left the RAF to work in civilian aviation. As Pullman wrote:

> The work he did for the RAF was concerned with pilotless flight. They used to tow targets behind pilotless aircraft that were controlled from the ground so that fighter planes could practice shooting at them. There was a civilian firm based at the airfield that was involved in that work, and he joined them and basically carried on doing what he'd been doing before.[15]

Pullman remained in Llanbedr throughout the remainder of his school years until he left to attend university. Wales boasted a proud heritage of independence from its powerful neighbor, England. The language spoken in Wales, for instance, was Welsh, a Celtic language related to Irish and Gaelic, not to English. Many people spoke Welsh at home and learned English at school. On Pullman's first day at his new school, Ysgol Ardudwy, his English accent got him into trouble. One of the boys asked where he was from. Pullman responded that he came from London. The next thing he knew, he was in a fight. About fighting at school, Pullman wrote:

> Later on I became friends with that boy, and indeed with most of the other boys I had fights with. I don't think it was a violent school, but there did seem to be a lot of fights in the playground. At one time I became anxious about it, and it was Grandpa who came to my aid. He'd been a boxer in his youth, and he showed me how to guard my jaw and jab and punch effectively, and from that time on, I knew I could defend myself. I'm sure he was right to do this. Fighting isn't the right response to bullying—for adults. Adults have to find out what makes the bully the way he is and look for reasons

and answers and understanding. That's an adult's responsibility. But children who are being bullied have enough to cope with; we shouldn't expect them to shoulder the burden of understanding and sympathizing with the bully's rotten home life at the same time that they are being beaten up. What children need most is the feeling that if they're attacked they can at least prevent themselves from being too badly hurt, and if the way to do that is to hurt the bully, so be it. However, I'm writing of a time when bullies used their fists. What you do to stop a bully with a knife or gun I don't know, and I don't think Grandpa would have known either. That's a different world.[16]

In *The Subtle Knife*, a book that was part of the His Dark Materials trilogy, Pullman wrote about a boy named Will. Will did in fact have to fight a young man armed with a knife. As Pullman wrote:

And the young man twisted over and reached for it [the knife] at once, but Will flung himself on his back and seized his hair. He had learned to fight at school; there had been plenty of occasion for it, once the other children had sensed that there was something the matter with his mother. And he'd learned that the object of a school fight was not to gain points for style but to force your enemy to give in, which meant hurting him more than he was hurting you. He knew that you had to be willing to hurt someone else, too, and he'd found out that not many people were, when it came to it; but he knew that he was.[17]

Although in real life Pullman was uncertain what to do in the face of an armed attacker, his experience with bullies and school yard brawls provided the background that he needed. He gave Will's fight realistic details of danger, pain, fear, and intensity.

Life in Wales was not all bullies and schooldays. In fact, Pullman had a type of freedom seldom available to children who lived in cities or large towns. He was able to roam the hills as quite a young boy, aged only 11 or 12. He explored, went swimming, and took walks by moonlight. With his friends, he built go-carts and rode them down the hills, recklessly endangering life and limb. One time the boys broke into an abandoned house, another they found fun in teasing a neighbor's pig. They hurled grass-bombs—clumps of grass and earth torn up by the roots—at each other, enjoying the explosion when a bomb splattered over an opponent's body.

For entertainment, Pullman's family might view a program on their television set. Television only came in black and white and had limited reception from two or three channels. At that time there were no satellites to provide hundreds of television channels, no videos, no DVDs, no home computers, no Internet, and no video games. Fast food consisted of fish and chips—batter-coated fried fish (usually cod) and French fries—seasoned with vinegar and eaten off of a twist of greasy paper. After homework was completed, children might occupy themselves with board games or card playing.

Reading was one of the evening time's main activities. Pullman's favorites were a mixture of English authors and books in translation. He wrote:

Among the "proper" books I loved, there are some that I still read. One is Arthur Ransome's *Swallows and Amazons*. Another is the funniest children's book ever written, Norman Lindsay's *The Magic Pudding*. And there were all the Moomin books by Tove Jansson; and another book I remember was a novel called *A Hundred Million Francs*, by the

French author Paul Berna. It was a good story, about a bunch of children in a dingy suburb of Paris who find a lot of money which has been hidden by some thieves, and all kinds of adventures follow.

The point about that book for me was that on page 34, there was a drawing of some of the kids defying the crooks, and I fell in love with the girl in the drawing. She was a tough-looking, very French sort of character, with a leather jacket and socks rolled down to her ankles and blonde hair and black eyes, and altogether I thought she was the girl for me. I wouldn't be at all surprised—in fact, now I think about it, it's obvious—to find that the girl on page 34 of *A Hundred Million Francs* is the girl who four decades later turned up in my own book *Northern Lights*, or *The Golden Compass*, where she was called Lyra. One more book: Erich Kästner's marvelous *Emil and the Detectives*.[18]

Llanbedr was too small to have its own cinema, so Pullman and his friends took the bus over to the next town when they wanted to see a movie. Movies from the late 1950s and early 1960s included *Gigi*, starring Leslie Caron and Maurice Chevalier; *Ben-Hur*, starring Charlton Heston and Hugh Griffith; and *Some Like It Hot*, starring Marilyn Monroe, Tony Curtis, and Jack Lemmon. In 1964, Julie Andrews starred in *Mary Poppins*, and Rex Harrison created the film version of Professor Henry Higgins in *My Fair Lady*.

One movie that Pullman recalled from his childhood was *The Magnificent Seven* (1960), starring Yul Brenner, Charles Bronson, Steve McQueen, and Robert Vaughn. These actors portrayed seven gunslingers for hire who are picked to guard a Mexican village from bandits. The bandits come periodically to steal anything the town has grown since their last visit. Although the seven were the underdogs, they decided not to run. They stood up to the vicious bandits in a climactic final showdown. The film was based on a Japanese samurai epic, *The Magnificent Seven*, acclaimed by many critics as the greatest Japanese film of all time. In an interview, Pullman compared one of the characters in *The Magnificent Seven* to the angel, Balthamos, from the His Dark Materials trilogy. Pullman said:

> Do you remember the Robert Vaughn character? He was the one with the fancy waistcoat, the one who's lost his nerve.
>
> There was a scene in the saloon where there are three flies on a table. He sweeps his hand across them, and when he opens his hand, there's only one fly there. He says, "There was a time when I would have got all three." Then the fight comes and he runs away, but he comes back right at the end and plays an important part.
>
> *The Magnificent Seven* has been with me for a very long time, since my boyhood, and when I think about it, Balthamos is playing the Robert Vaughn part.[19]

Movies were not always the main event of the evening. Instead, spying on lovers who were kissing under a bus shelter, or having a snack of fish and chips, might be more important than going to watch the film being screened. Most of all, the sense of freedom, the ability to be outdoors and on their own, appealed to Pullman and his friends.

One day, when he was 11 years old, Pullman was walking home from school when a motorcyclist passed him. In a few minutes, the motorcyclist came back and stopped near him. "There's a dead man up there," said the man. "I'm going to phone for help. I'm just warning you." Pullman thought about going home along a different path, one that

After returning to England from Australia, Philip Pullman spent most of his childhood in the small village of Llanbedr in Gwynedd County, Wales. Gwynedd County was made up of many other small villages, including Penmaenmawr (pictured above). Far to the west of Great Britain, on the coast of the Irish sea, Gwynedd County was popular with vactioners who enjoyed exploring the woods and rocky countryside as much as Pullman did. During his teen years in Llanbedr, Pullman discovered the freedom of the outdoors along with several lifelong intersts: art, poetry, theater, and music.

did not lead past the body, but the opportunity to see a corpse might never come again. He went to look, and wrote about the experience, "He lay quite peacefully on the grass verge. I suppose he'd had a heart attack."[20]

Pullman's family grew larger while they were in Wales. His stepfather's son from his first marriage came to live with

Pullman's family. In addition, Pullman's mother, Audrey, and stepfather had two more children, a boy and a baby girl. Pullman wrote, "So now I had one brother, one half-brother, one half-sister, and one step-brother."[21] Although he has written that at the time he did not see it, he now believes that his parents were successful at nurturing their blended family. The children had a wide variety of interests, and they grew up without resentments or sibling rivalries. As adults, they continued to get along well. Perhaps, as Pullman noted, they got along because they were so different.[22] He wrote, "There were differences of temperament, interests, age, background (where my stepbrother was concerned)— all kinds of differences. There was no conscious fostering of harmony; we had plenty of space to run around in and the parents left us alone."[23]

Blended families were very uncommon at the time. Divorce was a rare occurrence in the 1950s. Generally, blended families only occurred after the death of one parent. When the surviving parent remarried, as Audrey had done, children from both parents came together as blended families. Pullman wrote:

> But I didn't think very much about it; children think that whatever happens to them is normal anyway. The one thing that was slightly unusual is that Francis and I retained our father's surname, but I don't know whose decision that was. Often children take the surname of their stepfather. I was glad we were still Pullman; it didn't make any difference to feeling part of the family.[24]

In writing about his family, Pullman noted that his mother was not given the same opportunity for education that her brother was given. Girls brought up in the 1930s often did not receive much schooling. Audrey's parents had sent only her brother to school, not her. As a result, Audrey had an undercurrent of dissatisfaction in her adult life that was often directed at the children. She was very hard to please, he remembered in an interview. "She died before I had any success with my books. She thought I was a failure."[25]

As a teenager, Pullman began to wonder about religion and faith. As a child, he had believed his grandfather's teachings earnestly:

> So it [religion] was a very familiar part of my background and it was something that one didn't question. Grandpa was the rector, Grandpa preached a sermon and of course God existed—one didn't think of questioning it.
>
> Then, of course, I grew up and began to look around and see how people thought about things, and read books, and so on, naturally, I began to question this, as people do. And I eventually came—after a lot of swinging this way and that, and trying things out—to the position I hold now . . . Now, somewhere in the things that I don't know, there may be a God . . . But I can see no evidence in that circle of things I do know, in history, in science, or anywhere else, no evidence of the existence of God. Maybe there is a God out there. All I know is that if there is, he hasn't shown himself on earth. But going further than that, I would say that those people who claim that they do know that there is a God have found this claim of theirs the most wonderful excuse for behaving extremely badly. Whenever you see organized religion, and priesthoods and power, you see cruelty and tyranny and repression. It's almost a universal law.[26]

During his teen years, Pullman found several lifelong interests. He became engaged in the study of in art, poetry, theater, and music.

Art was a shaping influence on Pullman. He wrote, "But of all the things I remember from those years, the most exciting came when I discovered art."[27] At the age of 15, Pullman was given a book token (a gift certificate) for Christmas. He used it to buy H.W. Janson's *History of Art*, one of the classic introductory books in Western art history. The book, as he later wrote, remained in his possession for decades, although it became battered, almost falling to pieces. Living in Llanbedr, far to the west of London with its art galleries and museums, Pullman's art education came completely from books. He pored over the black-and-white illustrations and the few color plates in the *History of Art* constantly and "so intensely that I wonder I didn't scorch the pages."[28] The book provided the first inspiration in the visual arts that Pullman had received.

Pullman began to draw, mostly the local landscape around his home. In one of his books, *The Broken Bridge*, he wrote about a girl making discoveries similar to his about the landscape.

> . . . I drew obsessively, the landscape, mainly: the massive rounded hills, the wide pearly estuary, the tumbled sand dunes, the dry stone walls, the ancient church half-buried in the sand. I learned that landscape by drawing it, and I came to care for it with a lover's devotion . . . Many other strands went into the making of [*The Broken Bridge*] but what lay at its heart was love: it's a love letter to a landscape.[29]

Later, after studying English at the university level, Pullman realized that he had made a mistake. He believed that he should have gone to art school to receive formal training in how to paint and draw.

Yet literature, particularly poetry, provided a substantial source of inspiration for Pullman. Language captivated his imagination. He read poetry in school, from John Milton to

William Wordsworth to William Blake to the metaphysical poets. His English teacher, Enid Jones, encouraged his love of language, and under her guidance, she ". . . took me to places I had never dreamed of, places even brighter and more glamorous than Port Said, Colombo, and Bombay."[30]

John Milton proved to have a long-lasting effect on Pullman. He used a quote from *Paradise Lost, Book II*, at the beginning of *The Golden Compass*:

Into this wild abyss,
The womb of nature and perhaps her grave,
Of neither sea, nor shore, nor air, nor fire,
But all these in their pregnant causes mixed
Confusedly, and which thus must ever fight,
Unless the almighty maker them ordain
His dark materials to create more worlds,
Into this wild abyss the wary fiend
Stood on the brink of hell and looked a while,
Pondering his voyage . . .[31]

Pullman wrote that he received a physical thrill when he read Milton. In particular the passage below gave him chills:

High on a Throne of Royal State, which far
Outshone the Wealth of *Ormus* and of *Ind*,
Or where the gorgeous East with richest hand
Showrs on her Kings *Barbaric Pearl* and Gold
Satan exalted sat.[32]

Pullman wrote:

. . . my skin bristles; my hair stirs, my heart beats faster. I felt my body moving to the rhythm. When I first became aware that language could do that, that words had weight and color and taste and shape as well as meaning, I began to play with them, like a little child putting colored marbles into patterns . . . I learned enormous amounts of poetry by heart; I developed a great respect for craftmanship.[33]

Enid Jones's influence went beyond the introduction of Pullman to peotry. She was inspirational in organizing the class plays every year. Pullman felt that the plays were the most enjoyable part of the whole year at school.

One of Pullman's schoolmates, John Pugh, who was in Francis's grade at Ygsol Ardudwy, remembered Pullman and the school plays:

Did you know...

Philip Pullman admired the works of John Milton, especially *Paradise Lost*. Milton was born in London in 1608. His father was a scrivener (professional or public copyist or writer). His mother was extremely religious. Milton studied at Christ's College, Cambridge, where he wrote poetry in Latin. He traveled in Europe, where he met Galileo Galilei as well as other notable scientists, writers, and philosophers. When he returned to London, Milton founded a school where he taught for many years. He lost his eyesight in 1651, but blindness did not stop him from creating poetry. He dictated his works to his assistants, among them the poet Andrew Marvel. Milton was forced to pay a large fine for writing in opposition to the government. As a result, he was impoverished. He sold the rights to *Paradise Lost* for five pounds. He died on November 8, 1674.

These were a real treat and I was always very enthusiastic about participating myself. I also remember talking to Philip about jazz. To my surprise he was interested in this form of music at a time when not much was mentioned about it. I remember that I had been very impressed by a recording called "Time Further Out" by Dave Brubeck where the time signatures were unusual and I also remember that Philip asked me about a piece of jazz. He asked, "Would you say that piece of music was hot or cool jazz." I replied "hot" and he commented that I knew my jazz.[34]

During his high school years, Pullman was seen as the artistic type, and was known as "silly old Phil" for writing sonnets, for playing his guitar, and for painting. When the time came to decide what to do after school, Pullman took the entrance exams for Exeter College at Oxford. Encouraged by his English teacher to study literature, he was awarded a scholarship. Pullman was pleased and proud, even smug, to be the first in his family to go to university. Happy though his years in Wales had been, he left Llanbedr to study literature at one of the world's most famous universities.

After graduating from Oxford University, Philip Pullman moved to London in the late 1960s. Pullman discovered the excitements of city life while working and continuing to write. He also met his future wife, Judith. Pullman used Victorian-era London as the setting for several books, including The Ruby in the Smoke. *Pictured here is a busy street scene from London taken in the 1960s.*

3

University, Odd Jobs, and Marriage

THE UNIVERSITY OF Oxford, where Pullman attended Exeter College, was the oldest English-speaking university in the world. Although there is no exact date for the founding of the University of Oxford, teaching in some form at the site dates back to 1096. The university saw an increase in its number of students in 1167, when Henry II banned English students from attending the University of Paris. In the thirteenth century, the first residence halls were established to provide housing for students and scholars alike. Modern times have seen the university grow to over 17,000 students, with about 11,000 undergraduates. Women were first admitted to the university in 1920.

The University of Oxford acts as an umbrella organization for its member colleges, such as Exeter College, and halls. Any resources that the various colleges share, such as laboratories or computer facilities, are provided and maintained by the university. The University of Oxford also oversees the content of all courses offered at each college. Individual colleges accept their own undergraduate students from the applications they receive. Graduate students apply directly to the University of Oxford and are then admitted to the university itself. Degrees for all students, both graduates and undergraduates, are awarded by the university rather than by the individual colleges. Also, unlike college instruction in the United States, the normal course of study is a total of three years, not four.

Pullman began his studies at Exeter College in 1965. Founded in 1314, Exeter College was the fourth-oldest college of the University of Oxford. Exeter College was a small school, with about 300 undergraduates and 120 graduates. The first-year students all lived in the college dormitories and took their meals in the dining hall. After the first year, students were allowed to find off-campus housing if they chose to do so. Most students remained in the college residences on campus. The dormitories were close to the center of Oxford and they were reasonable in price. Students enjoyed living near the libraries and the dining hall. Social events were held close to the residence halls. Students often saw living in the college residences as an academic benefit. Living with other students nearby, who were in the same classes, made it easier to study together or discuss material from the week's work.

Exeter College used the tutorial system of study. In tutorials, students were taught singly or in pairs.

Students met each week with their tutors to discuss the week's reading and the essays they had written. The reading load was very heavy. The assigned essay was much less important than the reading. Many students found the tutorial system to be an excellent way to learn. Students who were good at absorbing large amounts of material and writing about what they had read generally did well in this system.

The tutorial system, however, did not suit Pullman. The emphasis in the tutorials was on how much reading had been done during the week, not on how well the essays were written. Furthermore, lectures, classes, and seminars were not seen as an integral part of learning. Pullman commented in his autobiography, "They existed, of course, but you didn't have to go to them, and it wasn't easy to find out where they were held, either. Nor did I ever find out how to use the library."[35]

Pullman's tutor at Exeter College was Jonathon Wordsworth, a descendent of the nineteenth-century poet William Wordsworth's younger brother. About him, Pullman wrote, "My tutor was an affable man, but he didn't like telling me that my essays were hopeless, so the only time he commented on my work was when, by accident, I wrote something good. I wasn't subtle enough to understand that: I thought it meant that I was doing well."[36]

Pullman had gone to Exeter College to learn how to write, but he found that his style of writing was not suited to the academic environment where the goal of writing seemed to be textual analysis or literary criticism. Later, when he began to teach writing, he did not follow the standard guidelines that called for heavy reliance on creating and sticking strictly to an outline. His writing, and his teaching of writing, was based on telling a story, not in arguing point after point after point.

Pullman did, however, enjoy life outside of the tutorial system. Rooms at Exeter College were organized around staircases. Each staircase was numbered according to its position relative to the central courtyard. In Pullman's second year, he lived at the top of staircase eight, next to a tower. One of his friends discovered that there was a gutter behind a parapet. If a student climbed out his window and along the gutter, he could climb in through a window further along the building. Pullman and his friends usually "did the gutter crawl" when there was a party on another staircase.[37]

Exeter College, located in Oxford, was in the same location geographically as Pullman's fictional Jordan College. Jordan was home of Lyra Belaqua at the beginning of *The Golden Compass*. Palmer's Tower, built in 1432 at Exeter College, also appeared in Jordan College as one of the oldest buildings in the fictional Yaxley Quad. Exeter College, like Jordan College, has developed in "a haphazard, piecemeal way, and for all its wealth, some part of it is always about to fall down, and is consequently covered in scaffolding: it has an air of jumbled and squalid grandeur."[38] Like Pullman, Lyra spent time on the rooftops of her college, although he noted, "I gave Lyra a better head for heights than I have."[39]

While he was at Exeter College, Pullman made many friends. He spent his time with them betting on horses, playing his guitar, drinking beer, and telling stories. One of the stories concerned the Bodleian Library. The Bodleian was an ancient, sprawling library that housed the second-largest collection of materials in England.

Did you know...

Philip Pullman and many other famous authors have made their homes in Oxford, England. C.S. Lewis (1898–1963), author of The Chronicles of Narnia series, and J.R.R. Tolkien (1892–1973), author of The Lord of the Rings series, both lived and taught in Oxford. While teaching at Christ Church College of Oxford University, Charles Lutwidge Dodgson (1832–1898), known most commonly by his pen name, Lewis Carroll, enjoyed telling stories to the daughters of the dean of the college, Henry George Liddell. These stories eventually came together in *Alice in Wonderland*. Clothing worn by Alice Liddell, Carroll's model for the character of Alice, is displayed at the Museum of Oxford. The town of Oxford and Oxford University are settings for well-known books and movies (many scenes from the Harry Potter movies were filmed there).

Philip Pullman wrote *Lyra's Oxford*, a short story set in the same universe as the His Dark Materials trilogy, as a guide to Lyra's world. The book comes with a fold-out map of her version of the city of Oxford, a short brochure for a cruise to The Levant (in the Middle East) aboard the *S.S. Zenobia* (a ship advertised in *Lyra's Oxford* as "the most up-to-date and comfortable cruise liner afloat"), and a postcard from the inventor of the amber spyglass, Mary Malone. The postcard shows some Oxford sites that are significant in Pullman's works and the map is useful in tracing Lyra's footsteps across Oxford.

Only the British Library in London had a bigger collection. As Pullman told the story, the library would have been Hitler's Chancery, if Hitler had conquered Britain during World War II. Underneath the main library, Pullman imagined, were numerous sub-levels and tunnels that stretched for miles in every direction. The levels were given letters instead of numbers to describe their distance under the surface. Sub-level L, the lowest one, was occupied by a race of sub-human creatures. Supposedly they got out and ran up the tunnels into the cellars of the surrounding colleges. Students who pressed an ear against a certain cellar wall could hear the creatures howling and scrabbling. Only the highest administrator of the university, the vice-chancellor, knew of their existence. The vice-chancellor passed the secret on to his successor, and to no one else, when he retired. Oxford inspired many flights of fantasy as Pullman and his friends embroidered their tales. As Pullman noted, "A great deal about Oxford is imaginary anyway."[40]

Pullman's description of Lyra's Jordan College reflected his undergraduate taste for phantasmagorical tales of the dark foundations of Oxford. In *The Golden Compass*, he wrote:

> What was above ground was only a small fraction of the whole. Like some enormous fungus whose root system extended over acres, Jordan (finding itself jostling for space above ground with St Michael's College on one side, Gabriel College on the other, and the University Library behind) had begun, sometime in the Middle Ages, to spread below the surface. Tunnels, shafts, vaults, cellars, staircases had so hollowed out the earth below Jordan and for several hundred yards around it that there was almost as

much air below ground as above; Jordan College stood on a sort of froth of stone.[41]

Exeter College was the home of another well-known writer, J.R.R. Tolkien. Pullman gave an account many years later of the time he met Tolkien. His description revealed Pullman's thoughts about fantasy and what he tried to accomplish in his own writing.

When I was an undergraduate at this college—this was Tolkien's own college. He was a Fellow here for many years, but he'd retired by the time I came here to read English. Now, in my day—I think it still goes on, but they might have stopped it now, I don't know—if you were unfortunate enough to read English at Oxford you had to study this filthy language, Anglo-Saxon, which we all hated. It's just full of barbarous, horrible sounds, and there's no literature in it, and all the rest of the stuff. That's what we thought then. So, we weren't very keen on Anglo-Saxon. Nevertheless, for some reason, the Rector of Exeter College was kind enough to invite me and two of my friends—all of us reading English—to dinner to meet Tolkien. This was in 1968, when everybody was being Hobbits, you know, we were all going about being hippies. He was pretty famous then. We went into dinner upstairs, in the Rector's Lodgings—thank God I was not sitting next to the old boy. One friend was sitting on his right, the other on his left. He turned to the first one—he knew we were all reading English—"Tell me," he said, "how are they pronouncing Anglo-Saxon these days?" My friend, who was as idle and ignorant as I was, could only sort of gasp and goggle. So Tolkien, slightly displeased, turned the other way and said, "And did you enjoy *The Lord of the*

Rings?"—to which my other friend had to say, "I'm awfully sorry, I haven't read it." So—well, I could've answered that question, but I couldn't have done the first question. So that's my Tolkien story: I have actually met him. But I've read *The Lord of the Rings*, indeed, but not for a while. So, what I'm getting at when I say . . . when I make what appear to be disparaging remarks about fantasy, are only functions of my ignorance of what the best fantasy is. Because my main interest, as a writer of novels, is in saying something which I believe to be true about the way which I think we are. I haven't . . . I didn't see that in Tolkien, and so I haven't read much fantasy since.[42]

Later in life, Philip decided that going to Oxford had been a mistake. "I enjoyed Oxford but it taught me absolutely nothing at all."[43] He felt that he should have studied art, and learned how to draw and paint. "But the way to that had been barred years earlier at school. Art was for those who weren't clever. If you were clever, you had to do Latin (i.e., follow the advanced curriculum that included studying Latin). I don't regret the Latin, but I do regret missing the art."[44]

It was at Oxford University that Pullman realized his goal was not to write poetry, but to tell stories. He graduated with what he called "not a very good degree," that is, not an honors or even a first-class degree, but a third-class degree. However, he had a plan. "I was going to begin a novel the morning after the last of my final examinations and finish it a month or so later. It was going to be published before the end of the year, and the film rights would be sold for a million pounds, and I'd be famous and rich, just like that. It was a good plan."[45]

Philip Pullman moved to Oxford, England, pictured here, in 1974 and began teaching at three middle schools. Storytelling became a key activity in his classroom. Instead of assigning reading, Pullman would tell the stories of some of the Greek classics—tales about gods and goddesses, heroes, and grand adventures. This brought history and literature alive for the students, and reciting the tales proved invaluable for his own writing.

To accomplish his plan, Pullman started writing the day after he received his degree. He bought a lined, 300-page blank book, and sat down to begin his novel. If everything went according to plan, the book would be done by the end of the year. It would sell millions of copies. The sale of the film rights would add to his wealth and fame. Instead, he wrote, "I was like the centipede who was asked which foot he put down first. I couldn't move."[46]

Paralyzed by the infinite possibilities that he might use to fill up the blank pages in front of him, Pullman wrote:

> What a shock! I had passed through the entire British education system studying literature, culminating in three years of reading English at Oxford, and they'd never told me about something as basic as the importance of point of view in fiction! Well, no doubt it was my fault that I got a poor degree; but I do think someone might have pointed it out. Perhaps it had been covered in one of those lectures I hadn't found my way to.
>
> What I couldn't help noticing was that I learned more about the novel in a morning by trying to write a page of one than I'd learned in seven years or so of trying to write criticism. From that moment on, my respect for novelists, even the humblest, has been considerably greater than my respect for critics, even the most distinguished.[47]

Faced with the prospect that his writing would not support him, at least not yet, Pullman moved to London. He found work in a shop called Moss Brothers, which offered men's formal clothing and evening wear on a rental basis. Moss Brothers was located in an area of London called Covent Garden, in the heart of the theater district.

Covent Garden was an exciting and colorful place to work. Designed in 1630 by the most famous architect of his time, Inigo Jones, Covent Garden was the first public square in England. Jones had studied architecture in Italy. He wanted to introduce the idea of a broad, open, central space into London. Until Covent Garden opened, London's streets were crowded, crooked, and narrow, a hodgepodge of unrestricted, unregulated growth. Jones's plan for the area featured the central piazza, with a grid of streets that ran parallel and at right angles to the open space. It became the site of the largest fruit and vegetable market in England, which covered the whole of the square and occupied many of the buildings. Nightlife was always an important part of Covent Garden. One of the oldest theaters in London, the Royal Theatre Drury Lane, was near Covent Garden, as was the Royal Opera House, the home of both the Royal Opera and the Royal Ballet.

The area around Covent Garden was redeveloped in the 1970s, but when Pullman worked there in the late 1960s, the fruit market still occupied many of the buildings on the piazza and the surrounding streets. Moss Brothers itself was a huge warehouse filled with elegant clothes. Pullman's job was to fill the orders, by pulling the right-colored, right-sized shirts, ties, collars, or trousers off long racks that reached to the ceiling. As he wrote:

To get to the top you had to climb through swaying lines of dinner jackets and trousers and tailcoats and morning coats. You could hide in there. At a pinch you could live there. You certainly wouldn't have wanted for food . . . One old man who was theoretically employed in the packing department never packed a thing but spent all his time smuggling watermelons, pineapples, and every other kind of fruit into the shop and selling it cheaply to the rest of us.[48]

Pullman's coworkers were a diverse group, the most diverse group he had ever known. They ranged from actors "resting" between theater engagements, to a number of Mauritanians, Australians, New Zealanders, and many other foreign workers. A group of gay men were the first confident, exuberant, proud homosexuals that Pullman had ever met.

While he worked at Moss Brothers, Pullman began a writing routine that became a lifetime habit. He wrote three pages a day, day in, day out, no more, no less. As he put it, "If you can't think of what to write, tough luck; write anyway, If you can think of lots more when you're finished with the three pages, don't write it; it'll be that much easier to get going the next day."[49]

At a party one night, Pullman met a woman named Judith Speller. They began dating, fell in love, and were married in 1970. Soon their first child was on the way. James was born in 1971.

By writing three pages a day, Pullman completed and published a novel. He later wrote that he would just as soon forget about his first book. He learned that it was not very hard to get published. He wrote, "Far more difficult, and far more important, was to write well."[50] The fame and fortune he had hoped to gain by his writing proved elusive. Although he enjoyed working at Moss Brothers, Pullman did not want to stay at the shop forever. He worked there for a year and then he found a job in a library. The library was more respectable than the shop, but in order to become a proper librarian, Pullman would need to get certified. Instead, he decided to become a teacher. His wife Judith was a teacher, and he liked what she told him about her students and classroom. Pullman enrolled at Weymouth College of Education and received his teaching certification. Soon afterwards, a teaching job became available in Oxford. The family moved to Oxford, where Pullman began to teach middle school.

Philip Pullman has always championed the art of storytelling, both in his teaching and in his writings. Here, he reads to a group of children at a London Zoo exhibition in 2004. The exhibition was based on animals in Pullman's His Dark Materials series of books. That's a lemur perched on his shoulder.

4

Teaching and Theater

PULLMAN'S TEACHING POSITION was split between three schools. At the time, in the early 1970s, teachers had vast latitude in deciding what material to present to their students. Teaching provided Pullman with a number of opportunities to use his creativity, talents, and interests for his students' benefit. He was able to tell them stories and to encourage them to write freely, without overemphasis on testing. At one school, he established a school library. Last, and perhaps most significant, Pullman wrote and produced as series of school plays while working as a teacher.

Pullman's family experienced one major addition. A second son, Thomas, was born in 1981. As Tom grew up, he became interested in science. His older brother, James, studied music and learned to play the viola.

Storytelling became a key activity in Pullman's classroom. He decided to tell his students stories from the Greek classics, stories about the gods and goddesses, about heroes, wars, and adventures. He used Robert Graves's two-volume version of the Greek myths, and prose editions of the *Iliad* and the *Odyssey*. The Greek myths included such tales as Jason and the golden fleece, Theseus, Perseus, the Minotaur, the labors of Hercules, and many more. The *Iliad* told the tale of the war between the Greeks and the Trojans, and of fall of the city of Troy. The *Odyssey* was the story of Odysseus's (Ulysses's) adventures as he journeyed home after the war ended. Both the *Iliad* and the *Odyssey* were written by Homer sometime before the Christian Era began.

Pullman spoke of his theory of how good teaching should include an increase in storytelling. At a lecture in 2003 at the Oxford Literary Festival, he said:

I want to champion teaching as telling stories: I think we should bring back story-telling into our classrooms, and do it at once. And I mean all kinds of stories: not just that every teacher should have a repertoire of fairy tales or ghost stories that they can bring out on a wet Friday afternoon, or when the video breaks down on a field study weekend—though I do mean that, and in spades—but true stories about historical events, about music and musicians, about engineers and engineering, about archaeology, about science, about the theatre, about politics, about exploration, about art—in fact stories about every kind of human activity . . . what any human beings can do who have lived and thought about their lives and about the things that mean most to them.

And when you're telling a story, you need to let the story take its own time. Never mind these programs and units and key stages; to hell with them. If the children want to go on listening, then go on telling.

And when you come to the end of the story, stop. Turn away from it. Let it do its own work in its own time; don't tear it into rags by making the poor children *analyze*, and *comment*, and *compare*, and *interpret*. Good God, the world is full of stories, full of true nourishment for the heart and the mind and the imagination; and this true nourishment is lying all around our children, untouched, and they're being force-fed on ashes and saw-dust and potato-peelings.[51]

It was important to tell the stories, not simply to read them to the students. Pullman taught three separate classes of 12- and 13-year-olds, so over the course of his years of teaching, he told the same stories again and again. He would take a whole year to tell the stories start to finish. Once he told a story to his son Tom, while the family was on holiday. Tom was having a hard time sitting still while they waited for their meals to be served, but Pullman's story held him spellbound. As Pullman recounts:

. . . when I got to that wonderful climax where Odysseus, disguised as a beggar, finally reaches his palace after 20 years away, to find it infested with rivals all seeking to marry his wife Penelope; and is recognized by his old nurse because of the scar on his leg; and gets Penelope to offer to marry any of the rivals who can string the bow of her husband, but no one can; and then Odysseus himself asks to try, and they all jeer at the ragged old beggar, but he picks up the bow and flexes it

and with one easy movement slips the string into the notch
and then plucks it like a harp, sending a clear note into the
shocked silence of the hall. . . . Well, when I got to that, Tom,
who'd been holding a drink in both hands, suddenly *bit* a large
piece out of the glass in his excitement, shocking the waitress
so much that she dropped the tray with our meal on it, and
causing a sensation throughout the restaurant. And I sent up a
silent prayer of thanks to Homer.[52]

Pullman had chosen the set of stories that are often
thought of as the basis for most Western literature, art, and
music. Common phrases have remained in use, which refer
to the stories. For example, the phrase "That's his Achilles'
heel!" which means "That's his weak spot!" came from the
story that Achilles's mother dipped him into the River Styx
to give him immortality, but she had to hold him by one heel.
The spot where she held him proved to be his undoing, for
Achilles was killed when an arrow was shot into his one
weak spot, his heel. Freud referred to the Oedipus complex,
based on the story of Oedipus, who killed his father and
married his mother. The word argonaut, meaning a sailor
who accompanied Jason on his quest for the golden fleece
on board the ship *Argo*, was the basis for the modern word
astronaut, meaning a space traveler.

As Pullman wrote:

. . . the real beneficiary of all that storytelling wasn't so much
the audience as the storyteller. I'd chosen—for what I thought,
and think still, were good educational reasons—to do something that, by a lucky chance, was the best possible training
for me as a writer. To tell great stories over and over and over
again, testing and refining the language and observing the
reactions of the listeners and gradually improving the timing

Did you know...

Little information is known about the man who is commonly believed to be the author of the *Iliad* and the *Odyssey*. He may have been blind; he may have lived in the sixth century B.C.; and he may have dictated his poems to a scribe based on legends he had learned as part of an oral tradition.

The *Iliad* tells the story of the Trojan War. Helen, the most beautiful woman in Greece, left her husband, Menelaeus, to run away with a young man from Ilium—more commonly known as Troy—named Paris. Helen is known as "Helen of Troy."

Menelaeus convinces his allies, the other Greek states, to start a war with Troy to recapture Helen. During 10 years of warfare, the Greeks were unable to take the city. Finally, they pretended to sail away, leaving a huge wooden horse as a present to the gods. The Trojans brought the horse into the city. When darkness fell, Greek soldiers who had hidden themselves inside the hollow horse climbed out. They opened the gates for their comrades, who had sailed back to shore under the cover of night. Troy was destroyed, although some of her citizens escaped and sailed across the Mediterranean to found Rome.

The *Odyssey* is the story of one man's travels as he tries to find his way home from Troy. Odysseus (Ulysses), as he is called, has many adventures, which include a trip to Circe's island, a fight with the Cyclops, and numerous others. When at last he reaches his home, he finds that a group of suitors, believing him to be dead, have been—and still are—courting his wife Penelope. Only Odysseus's old nurse recognizes him at first. This story is the one that caused Philip Pullman's son to bite through his glass with excitement when Pullman told it aloud.

and the rhythm and the pace, was to undergo an apprenticeship that probably wasn't very different, essentially, from the one Homer himself underwent 3,000 years ago. And the more I think about it the more grateful I am for the freedom that allowed me to think about what would be best for my pupils and to design a course that provided it. I wouldn't be allowed to do it now.[53]

Control over content and teaching methods was less stringent in the 1970s in England than it became later, with the introduction of the National Curriculum. The National Curriculum required specific tasks to be performed in specific ways with periodic standardized testing meant to measure how well the tasks had been performed. In an article in the *Guardian* newspaper published in 2003, Pullman wrote that he was concerned about "the mechanistic approach which seems to have taken hold of the way teachers talk about the process of writing. I'm thinking of the teacher who asked for my advice for her pupils who would shortly be confronted with a SAT (standardized academic test), where the rubric for the writing test told them to spend exactly 15 minutes on planning their story, and 45 minutes on writing it. Proper writing just doesn't happen like that.

"Nor does it always go through the process of planning, drafting, re-drafting, polishing and editing, which teachers are also required to put their unfortunate pupils through."[54]

In contrast, when Pullman taught writing, he told his students that there were no rules to writing, and that every piece of good writing had to be discovered in the process of writing it. His pupils showed him that his approach worked. He wrote:

[there was] the boy of 12 who was surly and uncommunicative, but who took a shine to me for some reason, and who responded when I encouraged him to write about the family's greyhounds. I told him to take his time, not to fret about it, but to talk to the page as if he were talking to me; and over half a term the most wonderful piece of writing emerged, full of knowledge and love and a vivid ability to convey it.

Then there were the two girls of 13 who wrote each other's biographies. Again, no pressure: they were best friends, and they wrote about how they went on holiday together, and how they chased boys, and how they argued and broke up; and then how the little brother of one of them died, and that drew them together again and now they couldn't imagine ever having hated each other as they once did so bitterly.

And those experiences of writing very vividly showed the children, firstly, that you could use language to say true things, important things; secondly, that what you wrote could affect other people, could move them, could make them think—"it affected me"; and thirdly, that you could work at your writing and learn to say things more clearly and strongly.

But none of that would have happened if I hadn't been able to give them the time to do it, and the freedom from the pressure of . . . Tests.[55]

Constant testing, timed writing exercises, and using a rubric that emphasized organization over inspiration detracted from the pleasure and spontaneity of writing. Having the leisure to write was important, as was learning to talk to the page just as the writer would talk to another person. Pullman compared the process of writing to fishing at night:

Writing a story feels to me like fishing in a boat at night. The sea is much bigger than you are, and the light of your little lamp doesn't show you very much of it. You hope it'll attract some curious fish, but perhaps you'll sit here all night long and not get a bite.

And all around you is silence. And plenty of time. You're in a calm state of mind, not asleep, not at all sleepy, but calm and relaxed and attentive: not the sort of heavy stupor you fall into after several hours' television, but the sort of unharassed awareness that we achieve when we're truly absorbed. True calm intense relaxed attention.

Are you going to find a fish? Well, there are things you can do to improve your chances: with every voyage you learn a little more about the bait these fish like; and you're practiced enough to wait for a twitch on the line and not snatch at it too soon; and you've discovered that there are some areas empty of fish, and others where they are plentiful.

But there's a lot you can't predict. Sometimes you'll feel a tug on the line and pull in nothing but seaweed; sometimes a cunning fish will flicker at the hook for a moment and disappear, with the bait in its mouth and the hook left bare in the water; sometimes a great fish will swim round and round, close enough to touch, and then with a flick of a tail plunge down into the deeps and vanish without touching your poor bait at all.

And the sea is very big, and the weather is changeable, and you really have only the most rudimentary knowledge of what things lie in the depths. There might be monsters there that could swallow hook, and line, and lamp, and boat, and you. These powers are not interested in any rationally-worked-out plans concocted far away on shore; none of the fish are interested in plans, or reason; the fears and delights of fishing at night have nothing to do with rationality.

So you set off in your little boat, your little craft of habit and intention and hope, and bait your hook, and drop it in the water, and sit and wait, calm and relaxed and aware of every ripple, every faint swirl of phosphorescence, every twitch on the line, until . . .

That's what it feels like to me, and that's only the beginning.[56]

Just as fishing at night could not be planned or measured, except in the eventual catching of a fish, writing could not be planned or measured, except in the eventual writing of a story.

For Pullman, as an English teacher, telling stories and teaching writing were very important. However, the most basic, fundamental part of his job was to encourage his students to read. One of the schools where Pullman taught in Oxford did not have a school library. Pullman was given funds to buy books in order to start a library. The 1970s was a rich time for children's books. Many books were being published with subject matter that had never before been addressed in books for young readers. Books that dealt with teenagers' feelings about their changing bodies, or books that showed young people questioning authority, were part of the new wave of realistic children's books. Pullman wanted to buy books that showed real children and teens in real situations with real feelings. However, some books, such as Judy Blume's *Are You There, God? It's Me, Margaret*, had been censored, or banned, at least in the United States. Pullman did not want to spend his limited funds on books that would not be read. He formed a parents' group to review several of his proposed titles. He gave copies of controversial, realistic teenage fiction books to the parents' group. Although some of the parents were shaken by the subject matter, they felt that the books treated the controversies with perception and sensitivity. Their positive response to the books showed Pullman that writing which described feelings about religion, sexuality, peer pressure, drugs, or other controversial topics could be read without objections or censorship.[57]

School plays provided another source of enjoyment for children at the schools where Pullman taught. He wanted the

While teaching, Philip Pullman also produced school plays for his students, as he felt it was important for children to experience the excitement of live theater. He later wrote several plays, including a version of **The Three Musketeers,** *adapted from the adventure novel of Alexandre Dumas (1802–1870). Pictured above is a scene from the 1993 film* **The Three Musketeers.**

opportunity to have his students act, and he wanted to entertain everyone, parents and students alike. He wrote about a protagonist called Spring-Heeled Jack, who had appeared in publications called penny dreadfuls. These books were melodramas that sold for a penny in the nineteenth century. Among the plays he produced were a story about Sherlock Holmes, *Frankenstein*, and *The Three Musketeers*. Another play was an original story called *The Magic Feather*, which was like the fairy tales from *The Arabian Nights*.

Pullman had an idea for a story that he eventually decided he wanted to use as the basis for a play. He thought that the story line would create wonderful opportunities for special lighting effects. As Pullman said, "I wrote the play to build up to this scene of flickering hellfire. It was terrific."[58] The play, titled *Count Karlstein*, is about an evil Count who makes a deal with the demon huntsman, Zamiel. Count Karlstein promises to give Zamiel a human sacrifice in return for vast wealth. When it comes time to turn over the sacrifice, Count Karlstein tries to escape from the bargain by giving Zamiel his two young nieces.

There was a serious side to the plays Pullman wrote, just as there had been with the stories he told to his students. Pullman felt that seeing live theater was very important for children. He said:

> Never before have so many people, including children, spent so long sitting watching other people pretend to do things. On the telly, of course. So I'm conscious that children, especially these days, with the television set in the bedroom, and so on, have enormous experience of watching drama. But it's drama on a screen. It's drama that is distant from you because of that. You can turn it off, you can flick the channels, you can turn the sound off. You can ignore it, because it's sort of separate from you.
>
> Now the huge importance of live theater is that you are in the same physical space as the actors. You can see the lights; the light that falls on them is reflects off them onto you—it's

the same light. You're in the same physical space; you hear their voices and it's the real voice you hear. They go clumping over the stage, you hear it. All the physical stuff, this is what a lot of children are starved of. They're starved of a physical engagement with the world. So when children go into a real theater and see real people doing dramatic things in front of them, there's an engagement that's almost visceral.[59]

Pullman also knew that watching a play was different from reading a book. He insisted:

When you are reading a book, you are in control of the speed you read at, and indeed even the order in which you read it. You are in command. Another way in which you are in command is that you supply the pictures when reading, you have to, so you're contributing.

When you're watching somebody acting it out, the visual stuff is done for you, you don't have to contribute that. And you are not in control of the time either. The play will start at eight o'clock whether or not you are in your seat, and you can't say, "Stop! Stop! Slower! Slower! Do that bit again!" So you surrender a certain amount of control.

But what you gain in exchange is the sense of a joint experience. You're experiencing it together with all those other people. When you're reading a book, you're alone, and there are great values in that. But when you're in a theater, and something transforming occurs, enchantment settles over the whole audience. That's something which you can't get by yourself.[60]

The importance of the plays Pullman put on was twofold. First, the parents and students who watched the play had the experience of live theater. They felt the unforgettable, visceral, shared experience that Philip believed was needed by a society of isolated television-watchers.

Second, the learning process was a benefit to the student actors. They enjoyed the sort of fun that Pullman remembered from his days as a star of student productions. He wrote, "It was the most enjoyable part of the whole year at school."[61]

Pullman had continued his habit of writing three pages a day during his years as a teacher. He wrote an adult novel, *Galatea*, published in 1978. *Galatea* is the story of a flautist searching for his lost wife through a series of surreal adventures. Although Pullman wrote that the book was hard to categorize, not being science fiction, nor fantasy, nor realism, it developed a cult following among readers. Yet it was in writing plays for children that Pullman found his life's work. He decided to take the story of Count Karlstein that he had written as a play and write a book based on it. Published in 1982, *Count Karlstein* was Pullman's first book for young readers.

Philip Pullman greatly admired Sir Arthur Conan Doyle, author of the books about the detective Sherlock Holmes. Pullman's play Sherlock Holmes and the Adventure of the Sumaratan Devil *was produced at Polka Children's Theatre in Wimbeldon, and then published as* Sherlock Holmes and the Adventure of the Limehouse Horror *(1993). Shown here are three of some 3,000 artifacts that belonged to Doyle. Included is the first known reference to Sherlock Holmes in a sketch for a book called* A Study in Scarlet, *a photograph of Doyle, and the name plate from Doyle's office in Southsea, England.*

5

The Ruby in the Smoke

PULLMAN'S LONGTIME INTERESTS included writing plays, as well as reading detective stories and other fast-paced, well-plotted tales of mystery and suspense. He had read and reread the adventures of Sherlock Holmes by Arthur Conan Doyle, which were set in the foggy alleys and byways of nineteenth-century London. Another detective story that Pullman enjoyed was *Emil and the Detectives*, by Erich Kastner. Penny dreadfuls, graphic novels that kept readers turning the pages at a furious pace with their melodramatic, highly twisted plots, gave Pullman images to use in the settings of his stories. Pullman combined many of the elements of the detective stories and penny dreadfuls that he had read to create his stage plays, and eventually his historical novel, *The Ruby in the Smoke.*

Three of Pullman's plays, *Sherlock Holmes and the Adventure of the Sumatran Devil*; *The Three Musketeers,* adapted from the novel by Alexandre Dumas; and *Frankenstein,* adapted from Mary Shelley's novel were produced at Polka Children's Theatre in Wimbledon, a town on the outskirts of London. As the theater's web site stated:

> Every year, over 100,000 children discover theatre at Polka . . . once they step through Polka's doors, their appetite for high-quality theatre will be powerfully awakened. We consistently set high standards for ourselves and raise the expectations of our audiences. We aim to deliver nothing but the best, which is what our young audiences deserve. We keep things fresh by discovering exciting new writers and dynamic new performers and by blending the best of contemporary culture with the finest traditions. Everything we do is focused on providing children with an exhilarating introduction to the incomparable magic of theatre.[62]

Polka Theater gave Pullman an excellent venue for his plays, produced in 1984 and 1985. He wrote:

> [Children] need to be helped into the experience [of live theater] by people who've been there before, and who can excite their curiosity. A little knowledge helps a great deal. A theater especially set up for children helps even more; and plays presented by people who know how to perform for children without talking down to them, or being facetious, or leaving their brains behind, are best of all.[63]

Pullman's play, *Sherlock Holmes and the Adventure of the Sumatran Devil*, was later published as *Sherlock Holmes and the Adventure of the Limehouse Horror*. Damp, grimy, working-class, and poverty-stricken, Limehouse, with its neighbor, Wapping, was part of the docklands by the River Thames. Pullman used the area, which was rich in history and rife with criminal activities, in *The Ruby in the Smoke*.

Having worked in Covent Garden, a part of London where many buildings existed unchanged from the late nineteenth century, Pullman knew both the city's atmosphere as well as the way street scenes would have looked. The Victorian Era, as the historical period was called, lasted from Queen Victoria's ascent to the throne in 1837 until her death in 1901. This period was marked by rapid expansion of England's international power. The British Navy became the strongest fleet in the world. Dominance at sea was followed by conquests on land, from India to Afghanistan to Hong Kong. Using her military might, Britain forced commercial treaties on her opponents that were favorable only to the British. One of these treaties regulated the trade in opium. Opium was controlled by the East India Company, one of the most powerful commercial enterprises in the world. Opium was grown in India, then shipped on East India Company boats to China, where it was traded primarily for tea and silk. The trade was immensely profitable, bringing in an estimated six million pounds per year.[64] By contrast, the Tower Bridge, which spanned the River Thames near the ancient castle known as the Tower, was completed in 1894 at a total cost of just under one million pounds.[65]

Opium played a role in *The Ruby in the Smoke*. Set in the same time and place as the stories about Sherlock Holmes or the penny dreadfuls, *The Ruby in the Smoke* featured a catchy, fast-paced plot like the Holmes stories. The inspiration for the novel came from two images. During the time he worked at the library in London, Pullman visited the antique shop next door. As he wrote:

> . . . one day I bought a couple of Victorian postcards, photo-graphs illustrating a sentimental poem called "Daddy," showing a little girl sitting on the lap of a man dressed as a workman. The idea is that the girl's mother is dead, and they're both sad about it; in the second picture you can see Mummy looking down from Heaven, dressed like an angel. I bought these two postcards for a few pence [pennies] and kept them on my desk for years without thinking very much about them, until one day I found myself wondering about the people in them, and especially about the other important person, the one who isn't visible: the photographer.
>
> And little by little a story began to develop in my mind, and the characters in the photograph came alive and told me their names, and the photographer emerged from behind the camera so that I could see him; and somewhere in the background, coming towards the studio, was a girl of sixteen or so, in terrible trouble. That was all I had to begin with.[66]

The girl in Pullman's mind's eye was Sally Lockhart. With the first book about Sally, *The Ruby in the Smoke*, Pullman wrote, "I think I first found my voice as a children's writer."[67]

The story Pullman spun about Sally, an orphaned 16-year-old living with an evil aunt in London, involves murder, opium smuggling, drug abuse, betrayal, friend-ship, love, and photography. At the beginning of the story, Sally's father has recently drowned. She goes to visits her father's business partner in the hope of finding out the meaning of a cryptic letter she had received.

When Sally asks if he knows the meaning of some of the words in the letter, the partner has a stroke and dies. With the help of an office boy, Jim Taylor; a photographer, Frederick Garland; and an actress, Frederick's sister Rosa Garland, Sally learns the meaning of the letter. An opium addict, Matthew Bedwell, provided clues to the mystery. Bedwell is also a riveting portrait of a man in the depths of slavery to drugs. The sinister history of the ruby from the book's title, as well as Sally's true parentage, are eventually revealed. Sally learns the truth about the death of her father. Throughout the story, the dingy atmosphere of Victorian London, where coal was burned to provide heat and to power the hydraulic engines that worked most machinery at the time, and where coal smoke polluted the air, was described in gritty, haunting detail. As Pullman wrote:

> Beyond the Tower of London, between St. Katherine's Docks and Shadwell New Basin lies the area known as Wapping, a district of docks and warehouses, of crumbling tenements and rat-haunted alleys, of narrow streets where the only doors are at second-floor level, surrounded by crude projecting beams and ropes and pulleys. The blind brick walls at pavement level and the brutal-looking apparatus above give the place the air of some hideous dungeon from a nightmare, while the light, filtered and dulled by the grime in the air, seems to come from a long way off—as if through a high window set with bars.
>
> Of all the grim corners of Wapping, none is grimmer than Hangman's Wharf. Its wharfing days are long gone, though the name remains . . .[68]

The abandoned docks, with their impoverished inhabitants, opium dens, disreputable boarding houses, bars, and warehouses full of streetwise orphans, provide a rich backdrop for Sally's story. When asked why he so often sets his stories in Victorian England, Pullman wrote that he found many parallels between that period and the current day, including new technologies, nationalism, feminism, and terrorism, to name a few. The language of the time made him feel at home, and as he wrote, "It was a time that was sort of balanced between the old and the new."[69]

Three more Sally Lockhart novels followed *The Ruby in the Smoke*. *The Shadow in the North*, published in Britain in 1988 as *The Shadow in the Plate* and *The Tiger in the Well*, published in 1990, recount Sally's adventures after the

Did you know...

An opium addict was one of the principal characters in *The Ruby in the Smoke*. Opium is a powerful drug that was used in the nineteenth century as a pain reliever. Because of its power to induce a dreamy, coma-like state, opium was also often smoked illegally by people seeking its intoxicating effects. Opium is not as frequently used in medicine today because of its strong addictive nature and unpleasant withdrawal effects. The principal character in Pullman's novel, Matthew Bedwell, became addicted to opium, and eventually died from the ill effects of the drug. The drug-induced trance he experienced was described with great skill by Philip Pullman, as well as the debilitating effects of opium on the addict's body.

dramatic ending of *The Ruby in the Smoke*. *The Tin Princess*, which features a character who had disappeared at the end of *The Ruby in the Smoke*, was published in 1992. About these books, Pullman wrote:

> Historical thrillers, that's what these books are. Old-fashioned Victorian blood-and-thunder. Actually, I wrote each one with a genuine cliché of melodrama right at the heart of it, on purpose: the priceless jewel with a curse on it— the madman with a weapon that could destroy the world—the situation of being trapped in a cellar with the water rising—the little illiterate servant girl from the slums of London who becomes a princess . . . And I set the stories up so that each of those stock situations, when they arose, would do so naturally and with the most convincing realism I could manage.[70]

The Sally Lockhart books were published over the course of seven years. During that time, Pullman also published a picture book, *Spring-Heeled Jack* (1989), based on a penny dreadful and on one of his plays. He also published three novels: *How to Be Cool* (1987); *The Broken Bridge* (1990); and *The White Mercedes* (1992), which was published in the United States as *The Butterfly Tattoo*.

The title character of *Spring-Heeled Jack* was a costumed superhero who had springs in his boots, a costume that made him look like a devil, and a burning desire to see that wrongs were righted. About the book, Pullman said:

> . . . I took Spring-Heeled Jack as my hero and just sort of wove a story around that. It's partly graphic novel . . . it's got speech balloons and it's got little poems; but it's got text in between. This I found quite hard to do, because there's a

curious thing that happens when you write a story in pictures; it is in the present tense, whether you want it to be or not. Pictures are in the present tense. But the text in between the pictures was in the past tense, like a conventional story. So there is a sort of disjunction, a not-quite-fit between the text and the pictures, which I never really solved.[71]

Pullman later wrote that he wanted to learn to draw better so that he could both write and illustrate his own stories. He noted, "I'm going to take some time to think about the curious and complicated relationship there is between words and pictures. Many people have written about this, but I seem to keep seeing things that other people haven't mentioned; so either I'm imagining them, or I'm onto something new."[72]

A longer work than *Spring-Heeled Jack*, *How to Be Cool* told the story of a dystopian society where the Coolmeter measured exactly how cool any individual was. The National Cool Board set standards for coolness and measured current trends so that manufacturers could cash in on them as quickly as possible. The story was made into a television show that was broadcast in 1988. Never reprinted, the book has become a collector's item, with copies selling for 10 times the original cover price.

Often, Pullman found himself writing his set three pages a day late at night. After a few years as a teacher, he began to write after school. His son James played the viola. Pullman found that he needed to escape the sound of the viola practice. He wrote, "[James's] playing was fine, but I need to hear the rhythm of my next sentence in my head before I write it. I can stand traffic, screaming kids, but not the competition of music."[73] He converted their garden shed into a writing shed.

The shed itself, originally nothing more than a place where tools had been stored, became cluttered with the odds and ends that are often found in a writer's studio. As Pullman wrote:

My shed is a twelve foot by eight foot wooden structure, with electricity, insulation, heating, a carpet, the table where I write (which is covered in an old kilim rug), my exorbitantly expensive Danish tilting-in-all-directions orthopaedic gas-powered swivelling chair, my old computer, printer and scanner (i.e. they don't work any more but I'm too mean to throw them out), manuscripts, drawings, apple cores, spiders' webs, dust, books in tottering heaps all over the floor and on every horizontal surface, about a thousand jiffy bags from books for review which I'm also too mean to throw away, a six-foot-long stuffed rat (the Giant Rat of Sumatra from a production of a Sherlock Holmes play I wrote for the Polka Theatre), a saxophone, a guitar, dozens of masks of one sort or another, piles and piles of books and more books and still more books, a heater, an old armchair filled to capacity with yet more books, a filing cabinet that I haven't managed to open for eighteen months because of all the jiffy bags and books which have fallen in front of it in a sort of landslide, more manuscripts, more drawings, broken pencils, sharpened pencils, dust, dirt, bits of chewed carpet from when my young pug Hogarth comes to visit, stones of every kind: a cobble-stone from Prague, a bit of Mont Blanc, a bit of Cape Cod . . . On and on the list goes. It is a filthy abominable tip (dumping ground). No-one would go in there unless they absolutely had to. I enter it each morning with reluctance and leave as soon as I can.[74]

Despite his protest about the unappealing working conditions in his shed, Pullman wrote 10 books during the decade between 1978 to 1988, although some of the books were published a few years later. In 1988, Pullman moved to a part-time teaching position at Westminster College in Oxford, where he taught prospective teachers. His courses included the Victorian novel, the traditional tale, and writing. He enjoyed working with great masterpieces, and found the contact with colleagues stimulating. As he wrote, "Writing has to be solitary, but I don't want to be a hermit."[75]

Pullman wrote two novels that are set in contemporary times. One novel, *The Broken Bridge*, Pullman wrote in the privacy of his shed. This book told a very different story from any of his previous works. Set in Wales where Pullman lived for 10 years, the story was largely realistic with some supernatural elements. The main character, Ginny, was the daughter of a white father and a Haitian mother. She learns that she had a white half-brother after the boy's mother dies suddenly and he comes to live with Ginny and their father. Ginny's quest to find the truth about her own mother and to discover her artistic voice was set against the beaches, towns, and hills of the Welsh coast. Pullman wrote, "I was really writing about my own teenage years in that part of the world, and my discovery of the visual arts, and my love of that landscape."[76] Pullman wrote about *The Broken Bridge* near the beginning of his autobiography:

My mother was hanging out some washing on a sunny day, and singing, as happy as a lark. The wind was chasing fat white clouds through the blue sky, and the sheets on the line billowed like the clouds, big fresh-smelling moist clouds that swelled and flapped and swung up high. The song my mother was singing filled the sheets and the clouds and the immense blue beaming sky, and I felt so light that I too might swing up and be blown along in the wild blue splendor; and she took me and swung me up, high up among the snowy-white sheets and the billowing clouds and the wind and the song and the endless dazzling sky, and I shouted and sang for joy.

Forty years later, when I was writing a book called *The Broken Bridge*, I wanted to give my character Ginny an image of perfect happiness; and nothing I'd experienced in all my life was better than the sheets and the clouds and the song and the bright blue morning, so I wrote about them in the same words that I've used here.[77]

The White Mercedes was Pullman's second realistic novel. The story dealt with sexual abuse, runaway teens, betrayal, and murder. Chris, the main character, made a choice between finding his lover, Jenny, or keeping a promise he had made to her. His choice, based on the premise that the end justifies the means, leads to Jenny's eventual death.[78]

In the early 1990s, Pullman began to work on an ambitious project. As many of his projects did, the story began with an image that came to him. Pullman worked in his writing shed, knowing that much of his effort would not be published. Yet every day he persevered, writing his three pages. As he wrote about stories in general:

Stories often start in that way: not with a theme but with a picture. An intriguing, puzzling picture, like something out of a dream, with scraps of intense emotion still clinging that seem to have no reason for their intensity. I write to find out more about the picture. For that reason I seldom make a plan before I start a novel. When I hear teachers telling their pupils that they must always make a plan before beginning a story, I want to hit them. In my experience making a plan first kills a story stone dead.

So I begin to write knowing that a lot of what I write—many of those three pages a day—will probably be thrown away or abandoned, because I won't know what shape the story should take till I've finished it. But I never think of it as provisional, a first draft, because, for the same reason, I don't know what's going to be important and what isn't. You have to simultaneously take the most craftsman-like care with every sentence *and* be ruthlessly ready to cut most of it out.

That's a state of mind I've found very hard to explain to non-writers. Often people who don't write have a mechanistic idea of the process: they think it goes through a series of precisely defined stages, beginning with "Get an idea," proceeding through "Write first draft," and ending with "Revise and polish." Well, it's not like that at all. The writing process is much more like what goes on inside a chrysalis when a caterpillar changes into a butterfly. The parts of the caterpillar aren't unbolted one by one and reassembled in a different order according to a manual: the entire substance breaks down into a sort of soup, and gradually a butterfly comes together, something utterly different.

Writing is like butterfly soup. Everything takes place at the same time, or rather outside time altogether. You're trying different titles at the same time as balancing the rhythm of this sentence with the one that comes after it and looking up the precise meaning of *vituperative* and wondering how to get rid of the murderer's accomplice and reading doubtfully over the first page and reading with pleasure over that good page in chapter seven and thinking that if you brought in the old woman at the very beginning it would be much more effective when she turns up later and finding out whether the heroine could have caught a train to Portsmouth before eight o'clock in the morning and wondering again about the harsh tone of the ending you first thought of . . . all at once: butterfly soup.

And what's more, you can't talk about it. If you slice open a chrysalis to see what's going on, you kill the butterfly before it's formed. So all this wondering and thinking has got to take place on your own in silence and in a sort of half-light of doubt and hesitation and uncertainty, among shadows that might become solid and might dissolve again into nothing. You have to become used to this twilight world if you're going to be a writer, and some people find it difficult to do that; they need the certainty of clear light and hard facts.[79]

One day, as he worked, an image came to him. He wrote about the experience of seeing the image for the first time: "[She] came to me as all my characters come to me, and I knew who she was at once. I knew what her name was and what she looked like, I could hear her voice. I didn't make her up. And I did make her up, but I didn't do it consciously. She just appeared. In the shed."[80]

The image that Pullman had in his mind's eye was that of a young girl, a child of about 12 years old. He watched and listened to her, and, as he wrote, he found that he had known her name from the very first that she had appeared. She was called Lyra.

Philip Pullman's books continue to be extremely successful. He has won several prestigious awards for specific works, including the Carnegie Medal for The Golden Compass *and the Whitbread Book of the Year Award for* The Amber Spyglass. *Two of his books have been turned into plays and a film adaptation of the His Dark Materials trilogy may be in the offing. Here we see Pullman receiving the Great Britons Award, 2004.*

His Dark Materials Trilogy

LYRA BELACQUA, NICKNAMED Lyra Silvertongue, arrived in Pullman's mind fully formed. As he examined her character, he soon noticed that she was not alone. He wrote:

> When I first saw Lyra in my mind's eye, there was someone or something close by, which I realized was an important part of her. When I wrote the first four words of *Northern Lights*— "Lyra and her daemon"—the relationship suddenly sprang into focus. One very important thing is that children's daemons can change shape, whereas they gradually lose the power to

change during adolescence, and adults' daemons have one fixed animal shape which they keep for the rest of their lives. The daemon, and especially the way it grows and develops with its person, expresses a truth about human nature which it would have been hard to show so vividly otherwise.[81]

What Pullman had noticed at Lyra's side was her daemon, called Pantalaimon. In Lyra's world, every human being had a partner, who could talk, move about freely, and change shapes as long as the human remained a child. The question of what exactly the daemons were produced much debate among readers of Pullman's works. One origin was Socrates' daimon. Socrates, the ancient Greek philosopher, was reported to consult a daimon and to listen to its voice. The Greeks believed that one's daimon was unique to each individual. It was a person's nature, the inner self that sought fulfillment. Another source for daemons was the idea of the guardian angel, a spiritual creature who guides and aids people in making good choices. Guardian angels, however, never appeared to anyone other than their assigned partners. Daemons, in Lyra's world, spoke aloud. They could be seen and heard by other people.

When asked what his own daemon would be, Pullman answered that no one can choose their daemon's final, settled form. He thought his might be a magpie, because of their fascination with bright shining objects, any bright shining objects. Magpies made no distinction between bits of tin foil or diamonds, but collected them all equally. Pullman referred to himself as a magpie of ideas, who brought all different kinds of ideas back to use in creating his storytelling nest.

In 1995, the first volume of Pullman's His Dark Materials trilogy, *Northern Lights*, was published in England. Titled

The Golden Compass in its American edition, the story tells how Lyra becomes the owner of a magical instrument called an alethiometer. She learns that many children, including her best friend Roger, have disappeared. Using the alethiometer, which she learns to read, and with the help of a talking, armored bear named Iorek Byrnison and her gypsy friends, she searches for Roger. Lyra discovers that her mother, Mrs. Coulter, is part of an evil organization that plots to use the kidnapped children and their daemons. The organization has discovered that by cutting the bond between a child and his or her daemon, enormous amounts of energy is unleashed. Lyra manages to rescue most of the children, but Roger is taken by her father, Lord Asriel. Lord Asriel performs a terrible operation called intercission on Roger, which severs him from his daemon and kills both child and daemon. The energy released by the operation opens a bridge between worlds, which Lyra crosses to follow Lord Asriel in the hope to repair the damage.

Two more novels set in the same universe followed *The Golden Compass*. The second book in the trilogy was *The Subtle Knife* (1997), in which Will, a boy from our world, encounters a window between worlds. After going through the window, Will meets Lyra in a city called Cittàgazze, the City of Magpies. He becomes the keeper of a knife that is so sharp it is able to cut the windows between the worlds. Back in our world, the children meet a physics professor and former nun named Mary Malone. Using computers, Mary is able to measure a previously unknown subatomic particle, which she calls "Shadows" and Lyra calls "Dust." Mary's work on Dust, and her meeting with Lyra, ultimately removes Mary from her placid professorial existence. In the third book, *The Amber Spyglass* (2000), Mary Malone goes to another world, one full of wheeled intelligent beings called mulefa. In that world, Mary creates a spyglass for viewing dust. Will and Lyra journey to the world of the dead in order to find the spirit of Lyra's friend Roger. They also meet the spirit of Will's father. They learn that Will's knife has unleashed a terrible kind of creature, called specters. Children cannot see the specters and specters do not harm children, but they suck the souls out of adults. After Will cuts an opening in the world of the dead, all the spirits are released. The book ended with a cataclysmic battle between the forces of Heaven, under the angel Metatron, and Earth, lead by Lord Asriel.

Pullman began working on the story about Lyra when he was 43. He finished it seven years and 1,200 pages later. After the first book in the His Dark Materials trilogy was published, Pullman stopped working at Westminster College in order to write full time. While he was working on the third book, *The Amber Spyglass*, Pullman was asked what his working day was like. He said:

I sit down to write by hand, in ballpoint, on A4 narrow lined paper, after breakfast, and work through till lunch with a break for coffee and reading mail. Then I have lunch and watch *Neighbours* (a television show). In the afternoon I read or take the dog for a walk or do something physically constructive (this summer I made a clavichord with my 16-year-old son—a delightful business for all sorts of reasons). In the evening I finish the three pages which is my daily task, or if I finished them in the morning, I do whatever journalism or reviewing or lecture-planning I have in hand. I spend Sundays answering letters; it takes me all day. I put the work on the computer after I've written it by hand. Actually, with the current work (*The Amber Spyglass*), my wife is entering the text for me, to save time, and I shall work on it when I've finished the whole thing, in a month or so.[82]

The titles of the U.S. editions of the books were created from physical objects found in the books. The object in the title of the first book, Lyra's golden compass, her alethiometer, is a truth-telling device. It takes its origins in a series of fortune-telling books that Pullman saw in a library in Oxford. When asked if the idea of the alethiometer was based on the Tarot, Pullman responded:

Not the Tarot specifically, but the notion behind or underneath the Tarot, yes. The notion that you can tell stories, you can ask and answer questions, and so on, by means of pictures. We come back to pictures again. What did influence it were those extraordinary devices they had about the middle of the sixteenth century—emblems, emblem books. There was a great vogue for these things. The first emblem book, I think, was published in 1544 in Italy. The idea was that you had a little moral . . . a little piece of wisdom encapsulated in a verse, usually Latin, usually doggerel, and a sort of motto, and illustrating those there was a picture. A favourite picture was a hand coming out of a cloud, holding a heart—no, two hands, one hand coming out of a cloud holding a heart, another hand waiting to receive it, and the hand waiting to receive it has an eye in the centre of its palm. Now the moral of that is that you receive a gift of somebody's heart, but first look, and make sure what it is that you're getting. So these were illustrations of trite and banal little moral points. Another favourite one was the helmet of a suit of armour, lying on the sand with bees flying around it. The idea of that is the things which once were instruments of war are now turned to peace. They're all rather everyday little things, like "look before you leap," or, "penny wise, pound foolish." Trite little, silly little, ordinary everyday observations; but, given this extraordinary semi-surrealist air by being pictured in emblem form in these rather curious little woodcuts. This was another source for the alethiometer—the idea that you could make a moral point or give information or whatever by using pictures. So I invented the alethiometer using a mixture of conventional symbols, such as the anchor, which is a traditional symbol of hope, and ones I made up, and I wrote out this long sort of recipe for how to use the alethiometer itself. And then I discovered, in a book of emblems in the Bodleian Library, something rather similar. It looked as though somebody had actually drawn the alethiometer. But what had happened was that in this particular emblem book, which was published in about 1620, somebody had invented a way of fortune-telling. You were supposed to cut this thing out, and you put a pencil or a stick through the middle of it, and you twirl it like this and, wherever it falls . . . you ask a question and you twirl it. Wherever it falls refers you to a number inside the book, and you look that up, and that's the answer to your question. So people were using this sort of thing in that sort of way. And then, of course, there's the Tarot, as you mentioned: there's the Chinese I Ching . . . all sorts of ways of divination. There are dozens and dozens of ways of interrogating the universe, basically, and the alethiometer is the one I made up for this book.[83]

Each of the books has its own new ideas and settings. The third book, *The Amber Spyglass*, contains the mulefa a race of creatures that is unique to Pullman's universe. Mulefa are intelligent beings with trunks who used seed pods as wheels. The pods, which drop occasionally from huge trees that grow in the mulefa world, have a hole in the middle. The mulefa are diamond-shaped, with hooked claws at the end of each limb. They hook two claws through seed pods and propel themselves by beating the other two claws on the ground. The mulefa shelter Mary Malone. After she learns their language, they help her make the amber spyglass. Using the spyglass, she is able to see Dust. Pullman wrote that the idea for mulefa came from a conversation with his son:

> The mulefa: I remember a day with my younger son, who was then 15, when we were on holiday in Slovenia, and we were speculating about the business of why no animals had wheels. What would be necessary, biologically, physiologically, for that to be possible? We were walking around Lake Bled, which is a very pretty lake all surrounded by trees, and in two or three hours we had invented the mulefa. At least, we'd got the creatures and the trees and the seed-pods and the wheels. But on their own they would have meant little and added nothing to the story; so then the connection had to be made with Dust and the basic theme of the story, which of course is the difference between innocence and experience.[84]

One aspect of the trilogy that caused heated debate among readers was the separation of Will and Lyra, who fell in love, at the end of *The Amber Spyglass*. In commenting on the book, author, teacher, and critic Marta Randall wrote:

> A major theme, running throughout the books and throughout all the characters, is that of responsibility and the importance of accepting responsibility. Lord Asriel and

Mrs. Coulter are both profoundly self-centered, competitive people until, at the last, they accept responsibility for their daughter and join to help her, even though they die in the effort and even though that effort is still tainted with their own selfishness and competitiveness. The sages of the Città world created a powerful weapon in the subtle knife, but lacked the responsibility to determine the consequences of that knife's use (unintended consequences are one of the banes of human existence). The results of this lack of responsibility threaten all of the worlds.

The theme is even seen in a minor character such as Balthamos, who falls so deeply into his own grief that he cannot continue his responsibility to Will—it is only at the end of the story, when he shoulders that responsibility again and stops the assassin-priest, that he can "join" with his beloved again.

There must not be more than the one remaining window, because if Lyra and Will leave a window for their own personal use, they would be behaving as selfishly as Asriel or Marisa or Metatron or the other forces that caused the problems originally. If they don't sacrifice their desires, they will not be fully accepting the responsibility they have taken on themselves.[85]

The book's conclusion, which declares that the republic of Heaven is at hand, along with the portrayal of the death of the Ancient of Days (the name used by the Prophet Daniel in the Old Testament to refer to God), caused some religious leaders to call for the books to be burned. Named "the most dangerous author in England," Pullman responded with an analysis of his philosophy. He included an explanation of how the myth of the republic of Heaven did what the traditional religious stories did. The myth explained why the world existed, and why we are here, as well as being a guide for understanding why some actions are good and some are evil. Pullman wrote:

> So a myth of the republic of Heaven would explain what our true purpose is. Our purpose is to understand and to help others to understand, to explore, to speculate, to imagine. And that purpose has a moral force.
>
> Which brings in the next task for our republican myth: it must provide a sort of framework for understanding why some things are good and others are bad. It's no good to say, "X is good and Y is evil because God says they are"; the King is dead, and that argument won't do for free citizens of the republic. Of course, the myth must deal with human beings as they are, which includes recognizing that there is a depth of human meanness and wickedness which not even the imagination can fully plumb. But it's no good putting the responsibility for that on a pantomime demon, and calling him Satan; he's dead, too. If we're so undermined by despair at the sight of evil that we have to ascribe it to some extra-human force, some dark power from somewhere else, then we have to give up the republic, too, and go back to the Kingdom. There's no one responsible but us. Goodness and evil have always had a human origin. The myth must account for that.
>
> But as well as the traditional good things and evil things (and there has never been much disagreement about those in all human history: dishonesty is bad and truthfulness is good, selfishness is wrong and generosity is right—we can all agree about those), I think we need to reinforce another element of a republican morality. We must make it clear that trying to restrict understanding and put knowledge in chains is bad, too. We haven't always understood that; it's a relatively new development in human history, and it's thanks to the great republicans, to Galileo and Milton and those like them, that

it's been added to our understanding. We must keep it there, and keep it watered and fed so that it grows ever more strongly: what shuts out knowledge and nourishes stupidity is wrong; what increases understanding and deepens wisdom is right.[86]

Morality, in the republic of Heaven, was the product of human free will, not the imposed unquestioned obedience to dogma. While some religious writers wrote very negative assessments of his books, others supported his belief in the spiritual quest, in questioning faith rather than blindly following the leaders of any church. Dr. Rowan Williams, the archbishop of Canterbury (head of the Anglican Church of England), said that teaching religion should include religion's critics. He wrote, "Clarifying objections is one way of clarifying what is being claimed."[87]

Pullman's works were often compared to the fantasy novels of C.S. Lewis or J.R.R. Tolkien. Pullman himself

Did you know...

Philip Pullman won the Whitbread Award in 2002. The Whitbread gives prizes in five book categories: children's, first novel, novel, biography, and poetry. In addition to the category awards, there is an overall prize for book of the year. *The Amber Spyglass* won the award both as best children's book, and best book of the year. It was the first children's book to win book of the year. Pullman did not expect to win either award, so he did not have a speech prepared.

expressed dislike of the two fantasy classics, going so far as to say that his books were not fantasy fiction, but that they were realistic. His argument for this view was that he portrayed real people in situations that showed their human conflicts and emotions. When Pullman analyzed the Chronicles of Narnia by C.S. Lewis, he found many objectionable elements, not the least of which was the unbelievable attitude towards the physical universe and towards death. In *The Last Battle*, the Pevensie children and their parents are killed in a railway accident. Aslan, the lion who is the embodiment of the Christian God, told them, "The term [school year] is over: the holidays have begun." Death was seen as the end of a particularly vile year at school. Life's end was the beginning of the summer vacation. As Pullman wrote, ". . . in the republic of Heaven, people do not regard life in this world as so worthless and contemptible that they leave it with pleasure and relief, and a railway accident is not an end-of-term treat."[88] Pullman's view was that life was not vile, and death was not the enjoyable state that Lewis felt it was.

In writing about J.R.R. Tolkien, Pullman cited the work of John Goldthwaite, a literary historian, whose *Natural History of Make-Believe* traced the evolution of fantasy in children's books. Tolkien, wrote Goldthwaite, created a world that was lacking in the real complexities of human emotion and psychology. Pullman referred to the Shire as the kind of plastic rendition of rural bucolic happiness that one might find in an Olde English theme pub. Fake oak paneling and reproduction horse brasses replaced authentic decorations. Not only was the world a pale imitation of life, there were areas that had been completely omitted from the narrative. In particular, there was no evidence of sexual feelings at all. Pullman wrote, "How children arrive must be a complete mystery to them." [89]

The His Dark Materials trilogy, beginning as it did with a quotation from *Paradise Lost*, showed Pullman's love of Milton's language as well as his interest in questions of free will, moral behavior, and obedience. As critic John Townsend wrote:

It is a powerful myth, expansive and absorbing. The evil figure of Lucifer, or Satan, in *Paradise Lost*, is now in the heroic role of rebel leader, but he is no simple hero: he, and his female counterpart, are deeply flawed and fascinatingly ambiguous . . . In *Paradise Lost*, Lucifer/Satan, having failed in his rebellion, makes a second attempt to defeat God, this time by tempting the first two members of God's new creation, the human race, into disobedience and ruin . . . Lord Asriel has the role of Lucifer. But Pullman has cast Mary Malone as the temptress: she tells Lyra, who is cast as Eve, of her first love and how it freed her from the church, whereupon Lyra is awakened to her sexual self and to love with Will. Here are the new model temptation and fall, and we are assured that they are "the beginning of true human freedom, something to be celebrated, not lamented." . . . In the clash between the Kingdom of Heaven and the Republic of Heaven, Pullman is ferociously partisan and gives no quarter. All the organizations of the Kingdom— the Magisterium, the Consistorial Court of Discipline, the General Oblation Board—are detestable; so are the individuals who staff them. But there is no outright victory in the war. It seems from the closing pages, when Lyra is back in Oxford and settling into ordinary life there, that things are continuing pretty much as before, with both sides free to fight again. [90]

The books proved extremely successful. In 1996, *The Golden Compass* won the prestigious Carnegie Medal, England's highest honor for children's literature. In 2002, *The Amber Spyglass* won the Whitbread Book of the Year Award. It was the first book published as a children's book to win the overall prize. In 2002, Pullman received the Eleanor Farjeon Award for his "crusading advocacy" of the children's book world.[91]

In 2004, Pullman, who had written several books based on his plays, now saw some of his books being made into plays. A two-part, six-hour version of His Dark Materials trilogy premiered at the National Theatre on January 3. The actors used puppets as their daemons; bears appeared in full armor; Will and Lyra journeyed by boat to the land of the dead. The books' transformation from 1,200 pages of text to six hours on stage required not only the technical expertise of the National Theatre's extensive stagecraft, but also a sensitive and talented writer to create the stage adaptation. Pullman found the work of playwright Nicholas Wright to be brilliant. Advanced ticket sales for the initial run of the show soared to a box-office record for the National. The production was revived in 2004, and it played to sold-out houses throughout the run that lasted into the spring of 2005.

Two other books, *Clockwork* and *The Firework-Maker's Daughter*, were made into stage productions. *Clockwork*, billed as "a spine-tingling tale of wolves, forests and a clockwork prince," became an opera for children age 8 and up. It played across Britain in 2005. *The Firework-Maker's Daughter*, a story of fireworks, a white elephant, and a girl who wanted to become a firework maker, played in Hammersmith before going on tour. In discussing the adaptations of his books into theater works, Pullman wrote,

". . . the thing that the theatre does best and most potently is to tell stories in a way that partakes of magic, of ritual, of enchantment."[92]

The film rights to the His Dark Materials books had been optioned by New Line Cinema. The award-winning playwright, Sir Tom Stoppard, was signed to adapt the books for filming. After Stoppard turned in his screenplay, a filmmaker named Chris Weitz was appointed to direct. He decided to make changes to the screenplay but stepped down as director in January 2004, citing his own lack of experience making large-budget, special-effects-intense, highly technical films. The option to make a film from the trilogy remained with New Line.

While His Dark Materials readers remained anxious for more stories set in Lyra's universe, Pullman wrote other works in the years after *The Amber Spyglass* was published. He retold the story of *Puss in Boots*, and wrote a book titled *The Scarecrow and His Servant*, published in 2004. A short but vital work about Lyra was published in 2003. *Lyra's Oxford* showed pictures of the hornbeam trees, a map of Oxford, and contained a new short story about Lyra. Pullman's work in progress, *The Book of Dust*, is the last work he planned to set in the world of His Dark Materials.

In his acceptance speech for one of his earliest awards, the Carnegie Medal (given in 1996 for *The Golden Compass*), Pullman said:

> All stories teach, whether the storyteller intends them to or not. They teach the world we create. They teach the morality we live by. They teach it much more effectively than moral precepts and instructions. The current campaign for moral education being waged by the Archbishop of Canterbury and

the Secretary of State for Education and Training could achieve all it wants in the field of moral education (and we all want a more moral society) by simply making sure that the schools' library service didn't die out. Give the books to the teachers, and then leave them alone; give them time to read and think and talk about the books with one another and with their students, so that they can put the right book into the hands of the right child at the right time.

We don't need lists of rights and wrongs, tables of do's and don'ts: we need books, time, and silence. Thou shalt not is soon forgotten, but Once upon a time lasts forever.[93]

1 Philip Pullman, "About the Author: I have a feeling this all belongs to me," *www.philip-pullman.com/pages/content/index.asp?PageID=84.*

2 Ibid.

3 Ibid.

4 Ibid.

5 His Dark Materials | Philip Pullman, About the Author, *www.randomhouse.com/features/pullman/philippullman/index.html.*

6 Margaret Speaker Yuan's email with Philip Pullman, January 15, 2005.

7 Philip Pullman, "About the Author: I have a feeling this all belongs to me."

8 Ibid.

9 Ibid.

10 Ibid.

11 Ibid.

12 Ibid.

13 Ibid.

14 Ibid.

15 Margaret Speaker Yuan's email with Philip Pullman, January 15, 2005.

16 Philip Pullman, "About the Author: I have a feeling this all belongs to me."

17 Philip Pullman, *The Subtle Knife* (New York: Knopf, 1977), 174.

18 Philip Pullman, "About the Writing," *www.philip-pullman.com/about_the_writing.asp.*

19 Dave Welch, "Philip Pullman Reaches the Garden," Powells.com Interviews–Philip Pullman (2000), August 31, 2000, *www.powells.com/authors/pullman.html.*

20 Philip Pullman, "About the Author: I have a feeling this all belongs to me."

21 Ibid.

22 Ibid.

23 Margaret Speaker Yuan's email with Philip Pullman, January 15, 2005.

24 Margaret Speaker Yuan's email with Philip Pullman, January 15, 2005.

25 Dina Rabinovitch, Guardian Unlimited Books | By genre | Interview: Philip Pullman, *His Bright Materials*, December 10, 2003, *http://books.guardian.co.uk/departments/childrenandteens/story/0,6000,1103616,00.html.*

26 Susan Roberts, *A Dark Agenda?*, Sure Fish, November 2002, *www.surefish.co.uk/culture/features/pullman_interview.htm.*

27 Philip Pullman, "About the Author: I have a feeling this all belongs to me."

28 Ibid.

29 Ibid.

30 Ibid.

31 John Milton, Paradise Lost–Book 2, ll. 910–919, *www.dartmouth.edu/~milton/reading_room/pl/book_2/index.shtml.*

32 Ibid., ll. 1–5

33 Philip Pullman, "About the Author: I have a feeling this all belongs to me."

34 Margaret Speaker Yuan's email with John Pugh, December 22, 2004.

35 Philip Pullman, "About the Author: I have a feeling this all belongs to me."

36 Ibid.

37 Guardian Unlimited Books | Review | Philip Pullman: Dreaming of spires, July 27, 2002, *http://books.guardian.co.uk/review/story/0,12084,763709,00.html*.

38 Ibid.

39 Ibid.

40 Ibid.

41 Pullman, Philip, *The Golden Compass* (New York: Knopf, 1995) 48.

42 T. Brown, Interview with Philip Pullman, August 2000, *www.avnet.co.uk/amaranth/Critic/ivpullman.htm*.

43 Margaret Speaker Yuan's email with Philip Pullman, January 15, 2005.

44 Philip Pullman, "About the Author: I have a feeling this all belongs to me."

45 Ibid.

46 Ibid.

47 Ibid.

48 Ibid.

49 Ibid.

50 Ibid.

51 Philip Pullman, "About the Worlds: Education: Isis Speech," *www.philip-pullman.com/pages/content/index.asp?PageID=66*.

52 Philip Pullman, "About the Author: I have a feeling this all belongs to me."

53 Ibid.

54 Mira Katbamna, EducationGuardian.co.uk | News crumb | Lost the plot, September 30, 2003, *http://education.guardian.co.uk/schools/story/0,5500,1052077,00.html*.

55 Ibid.

56 Philip Pullman, "About the Worlds: Education: Isis Speech."

57 Nicholas Tucker, *Darkness Visible: Inside the World of Philip Pullman* (London, U.K.: Wizard Books, 2003), 21.

58 Robert Butler. *The Art of Darkness: Staging the Philip Pullman Trilogy* (London, U.K.: Oberon Books, 2003), 35.

59 Butler, 35.

60 Butler, 37.

61 Butler, 33.

62 Polka Theater Web Site, About Polka Theatre, *www.polkatheatre.com/about_company.asp*.

63 Philip Pullman, EducationGuardian.co.uk | eG weekly | Theatre - the true key stage, March 30, 2004, *http://education.guardian.co.uk/egweekly/story/0,5500,1180330,00.html*.

64 The Maritime Trust, The Maritime Heritage Project: Maritime History of Gold Rush Ships, Captains, Passengers, News–Opium, *www.maritime-heritage.org/newtale/opium.html*.

65 Margaret Speaker Yuan, *The London Tower Bridge* (Farmington Hills, MI: Blackbirch Press, 2004), 39.

66 Philip Pullman, "About the Author: I have a feeling this all belongs to me."

67 Ibid.

68 Pullman, Philip, *The Ruby in the Smoke* (New York: Knopf , 1985), 20.

69 Philip Pullman, *Newsmakers*, Issue 2 (Farmington Hills, MI: Gale Group, 2003). Reproduced in *Student Resource Center* (Detriot, MI: Gale, 2004).

70 Philip Pullman, "About the Books: The Sally Lockhart quartet," *www.philip-pullman.com/pages/content/index.asp?PageID=28.*

71 Brown, Interview with Philip Pullman, August 2000.

72 Philip Pullman, "About the Author: I have a feeling this all belongs to me."

73 John Cornwell, Some enchanted author - Sunday Times - Times Online, October 24, 2004, *www.timesonline.co.uk/article/0,,2099-1311328,00.html.*

74 ACHUKA–Philip Pullman, *www.achuka.co.uk/archive/interviews/ppint.php.*

75 Philip Pullman, "About the Author: I have a feeling this all belongs to me."

76 Philip Pullman, "About the Books: Contemporary Novels: *The Broken Bridge*," *www .philip-pullman.com/pages/content/index.asp?PageID=34.*

77 Philip Pullman, "About the Author: I have a feeling this all belongs to me."

78 Tucker, 83.

79 Philip Pullman, "About the Author: I have a feeling this all belongs to me."

80 Sally Vincent, Guardian Unlimited | The Guardian | Driven by daemons, November 10, 2001, *www.guardian.co.uk/weekend/story/0,,589797,00.html.*

81 Author Interview–Philip Pullman, January 2004, *www.jubileebooks.co.uk/jubilee/magazine/authors/philip_pullman/interview.asp.*

82 ACHUKA–Philip Pullman.

83 Brown, Interview with Philip Pullman, August 2000.

84 Marta Randall, Online Chat with Philip Pullman, February 5–9, 2001, *www.readerville.com/webx?50*

85 Ibid.

86 Philip Pullman, "The Republic of Heaven," *Horn Book Magazine* (November/December 2001) Vol. 77, Issue 6, 655–668.

87 Ronan McGreevy, Archbishop wants atheist Pullman on syllabus–Home–Times Online, March 9, 2004, *www.timesonline.co.uk/article/0,,1-1031866,00.html.*

88 Philip Pullman, "The Republic of Heaven."

89 Ibid.

90 John Rowe Townsend, "Paradise Reshaped," *Horn Book Magazine* (July/August 2002) Vol. 78, Issue 5, 415–421.

91 Booktrusted.com–information and advice about children's, *www.booktrusted.co.uk/prizes/prizes.php4?action=2&przid=128.*

92 Philip Pullman, "About the Author: Essays and Articles: Children's Theatre," *www.philip-pullman.com/pages/content/index.asp?PageID=106.*

93 Philip Pullman, His Dark Materials | Philip Pullman | Carnegie Medal Acceptance Speech, November 27, 1996, *www.randomhouse.com/features/pullman/philippullman/speech.html.*

1946 Born October 19 in Norwich, England, son of Alfred and Audrey Pullman.

1954 Alfred killed in action in Kenya. Pullman and brother Francis live with their grandparents, Reverend and Mrs. Merrifield, in Norfolk, England.

1955 Audrey remarries; the family moves to Australia.

1957 Family moves to Llanbedr.

1965 Graduates from Ygsol Ardudwy; goes to Oxford to attend Exeter College at the University of Oxford.

1968 Receives Bachelor of Arts degree from the University of Oxford; moves to London.

1970 Marries Judith Speller, August 15.

1971 Son James Pullman is born.

1972 *The Haunted Storm* published.

1974 Obtains a teaching certificate, moves to Oxford, begins teaching at three middle schools in Oxford: Ivanhoe, Bishop Kirk, and Marston.

1978 Publishes *Galatea* and *Ancient Civilizations*.

1981 Son Thomas Pullman is born.

1982 Publishes *Count Karlstein*.

1984 *Sherlock Holmes and the Adventure of the Sumatran Devil* is produced at Polka Children's Theatre, Wimbledon.

1985 *Three Musketeers* (adapted from Alexandre Dumas' novel of the same title) is produced at Polka Children's Theatre, Wimbledon. Publishes *The Ruby in the Smoke*.

1987 *How to Be Cool* published. *Frankenstein* (adapted from Mary Shelley's novel of the same title) produced at Polka Children's Theatre, Wimbledon.

1988 *The Shadow in the Plate* published. *The Shadow in the North* published (U.S. edition of *The Shadow in the Plate*). Obtained position as part-time lecturer at Westminster College—holds the post for the next eight years.

1989 *Penny Dreadful* and *Spring-Heeled Jack* published.

1990 *Frankenstein* (adapted from Mary Shelley's novel of the same title), *The Tiger in the Well*, and *The Broken Bridge* published.

1992 *The White Mercedes* and *The Tin Princess* published.

1993 *Sherlock Holmes and the Adventure of the Limehouse Horror* published.

1994 *Thunderbolt's Waxworks* published.

1995 *Northern Lights* and *The Gas-Fitter's Ball* published.

1996 *The Golden Compass* (U.S. edition of *Northern Lights*), *Clockwork; or, All Wound Up*, and *The Firework-Maker's Daughter* published.

1997 *The Subtle Knife* published. *Puss in Boots* produced at Polka Children's Theatre, Wimbledon.

2000 *The Amber Spyglass, I Was a Rat*, and *Puss In Boots* published.

2002 *Count Karlstein–The Novel* published.

2003 *Lyra's Oxford* published. Pullman is named a Commander of the British Empire.

2004 *The Scarecrow and His Servant* published. His Dark Materials trilogy stage play opens at the National Theatre. *Aladdin and the Enchanted Lamp* reissued.

2005 *The Book of Dust* is a work in progress.

CLOCKWORK

The townspeople of Glockenheim gather in the White Horse Tavern. Fritz, a young storyteller, has a new tale to tell. The clockwork-maker's apprentice, Karl, confides in Fritz that he has been unable to complete a new figure for the town clock. Karl is afraid that he will become the first apprentice in centuries to fail at his task. Karl is offered a clockwork figure to use by the evil Dr. Kalmenius.

THE GOLDEN COMPASS

This is the first book in the His Dark Materials triolgy. Lyra Belacqua leaves her home in Oxford to find her friend Roger Parslow, who has been kidnapped. Before she leaves, she receives an alethiometer, a kind of compass that tells the truth when she asks it questions. She learns the truth of her parentage, and rescues a number of children who were kidnapped. Her father, Lord Asrial, performs an abominable operation on Roger, which kills the boy. The energy released by the operation opens a window between worlds. Lyra passes through it into a new universe.

THE SUBTLE KNIFE

This is the second book in the His Dark Materials trilogy. Will, a boy from our Oxford, finds a window between worlds. He goes through it and meets Lyra. He receives a knife that is so sharp it can cut windows between worlds. Together, they set out to find Will's father.

THE AMBER SPYGLASS

This is the last of the His Dark Materials triolgy. Mary Malone, a researcher from our Oxford, goes through the same window that Will went through. She finds another window and enters a world where intelligent beings called mulefa propel themselves using wheels that fit on their claws. Mary makes a special spyglass that sees what she calls shadows, and the mulefa call sraf. This substance is the key to consciousness. She encounters Will and Lyra, whom she had met in our world in the previous book. The children help free the dead, who were imprisoned in a dark universe without an escape. They witness Lord Asrial's assault on the Authority, and see its death.

THE FIREWORK-MAKER'S DAUGHTER

Lila, the firework-maker's daughter, wants to follow in her father's footsteps and become a master firework-maker. He thinks she should take a girl's traditional role and find herself a husband. With the help of her Chulak, the personal servant to the king's talking white elephant, Lila learns that to be a true firework-maker, she must face down the Fire-Fiend of Mount Merapi and bring back the royal sulphur. She sets off, but the way to Mount Merapi is full of danger. The final danger is the Fire-Fiend himself.

THE RUBY IN THE SMOKE

In search of clues to a mysterious letter that refers to her father's death, 16-year-old Sally Lockhart contacts her father's partner. The mention of some words from the letter brings on a fatal heart attack for the partner. Sally finds further clues, and learns the truth about her father's death, as well as about her parentage, and about a ruby that was coveted by many people who were not afraid to kill in order to own it.

THE SHADOW IN THE NORTH

This is the sequel to *The Ruby in the Smoke.* Sally, now 22, is in business as a financial consultant. When she and her friends challenge corrupt financial interests, they find themselves entangled in a series of deceptions that connects a magician, a beautiful young girl, one of Sally's clients, and the wealthiest man in Europe.

THE TIGER IN THE WELL

This is the third book about Sally Lockhart. Sally is now a young woman, the single mother of a baby who was fathered by her dead lover, Frederick Garland. A man she has never met or even heard of sues her for divorce and custody of her daughter. Sally struggles to keep her daughter and unravel the secrets of her mysterious persecutor.

1972 *The Haunted Storm*

1978 *Ancient Civilizations, Galatea*

1982 *Count Karlstein*

1985 *The Ruby in the Smoke*

1987 *How to Be Cool, The Shadow in the Plate*

1988 *The Shadow in the North*

1989 *Penny Dreadful, Spring-Heeled Jack*

1990 *Frankenstein, The Tiger in the Well, The Broken Bridge*

1992 *The White Mercedes, The Tin Princess*

1993 *Sherlock Holmes and the Adventure of the Limehouse Horror*

1994 *Thunderbolt's Waxworks*

1995 *Northern Lights, The Gas-Fitter's Ball*

1996 *The Golden Compass, Clockwork; or, All Wound Up, The Firework-Maker's Daughter*

1997 *The Subtle Knife*

2000 *The Amber Spyglass, I Was a Rat, Puss In Boots*

2002 *Count Karlstein–The Novel*

2003 *Lyra's Oxford*

2004 *The Scarecrow and His Servant, Aladdin and the Enchanted Lamp*

LORD ASRIEL

Lord Asriel is Lyra Belacqua's father. He mounts a war against the Authority. In order to do so, he needs huge amounts of energy. He severs Lyra's friend Roger from his daemon in order to create the power he needs.

LYRA BELACQUA AND PANTALAIMON

Lyra and her daemon Pantalaimon become the owner of a truth-telling instrument called an alethiometer. Lyra learns that children, including her friend Roger Parslow, are being kidnapped. She uses the alethiometer to find out where they are being taken. With the help of Iorik Byrnison and Serafina Pekkala, she rescues Roger.

IOREK BYRNISON

An armored bear, Iorek takes Lyra to the north to find the kidnapped children. He reforges the Subtle Knife when Will accidentally breaks it. Iorek helps in the final battle between the forces of the Authority and Lord Asriel.

MRS. MARISA COULTER

Lyra's mother, Mrs. Coulter is responsible for the kidnapping of many children, including Roger Parslow. She performs repulsive experiments on the children, severing them from their daemons.

FREDERICK GARLAND

A photographer, Frederick befriends Sally Lockhart. He later becomes a detective. He falls in love with Sally, becomes her lover, but dies before they can marry. He is the father of her child.

MRS. MOLLY HOLLAND

The evil Mrs. Holland kills Sally's true father and tries to steal the ruby. She forces opium on one of her lodgers in an attempt to get him to reveal where the ruby is hidden. She tries to kill Sally but ends up throwing herself off the London Bridge when Sally tosses the ruby off the bridge and into the River Thames below.

LALCHUND

Lalchund is the firework-maker, Lila's father. He teaches Lila the techniques of making fireworks, but does not tell her the three secrets. He was imprisoned by the king and forced to compete with other firework-makers to see who is the best in the world. He and Lila win the competition, and his life is spared.

LILA

Lila is the title character in *The Firework-Maker's Daughter*. She wants to become a firework-maker, but her father refuses to tell her the secrets she would need to become one. She travels to the pit of the Fire Fiend to bring back the royal sulphur, which she believed would let her become a master firework-maker.

SALLY LOCKHART

Sally Lockhart, a girl of 16, discovers a mystery about her father's death. In order to solve it, she has to unravel a series of clues and face many dangerous situations. A gigantic ruby, opium, and photography featured in a fast-paced melodrama set in Victorian England.

MARY MALONE

An Oxford physicist and former nun, Mary helps Lyra learn about the subatomic particle (called shadows by Mary and Dust by people from Lyra's world). She goes through Will's window into another world. After traveling through that world, she finds another window. When she goes through the second window, she meets a race of beings called mulefa. With their help, she builds a spyglass to see Dust.

WILL PARRY

Will discovers a window between the worlds. He goes through it and finds Lyra. Together, they go to Oxford to find out more about Will's father. Will becomes the keeper of the subtle knife, a knife so sharp it can cut windows between the worlds.

ROGER PARSLOW

Roger is Lyra's friend from Oxford. His kidnapping causes Lyra to go to the North to try to rescue him. He is killed when Lord Asriel severs his daemon from him. Lyra finds his spirit in the world of the dead.

SERAFINA PEKKALA

A witch, Serafina helps Lyra rescue the kidnapped children from the experiments performed by Mrs. Coulter and her organization. After the energy unleashed by Roger's death opens a bridge between worlds, Serafina crosses it to continue helping Lyra.

LEE SCORESBY

A Texan and an aeronaut, Lee also helps Lyra rescue the imprisoned children. Lee goes on to help Will find his father. He dies protecting Lyra.

JIM TAYLOR

Jim is an office boy who works for the shipping firm owned by Sally's father. When she receives a cryptic note about her father's death, he helps her solve the mystery. He becomes Frederick's assistant.

1987 Lancashire County Libraries/National and Provincial Children's Book Award, Best Books for Young Adults citation, *School Library Journal.*

1988 Children's Book Award, International Reading Association, for *The Ruby in the Smoke.* Best Books for Young Adults citation, American Library Association (ALA), for *The Ruby in the Smoke.* Preis der Leseratten, ZDF Television (Germany) for *The Ruby in the Smoke.* Best Books for Young Adults citation, ALA.

1989 Edgar Allan Poe Award nomination, Mystery Writers of America, for *Shadow in the North.*

1996 Carnegie Medal, British Library Association, for *Northern Lights. Publishing News* British Children's Book of the Year Award, for *Northern Lights.* Children's Fiction Award, *Guardian,* all 1996, for *Northern Lights.* Smarties Gold Award, Rowntree Mackintosh Co., for *The Firework Maker's Daughter.* Carnegie Medal short-list, British Library Association, *Clockwork, or All Wound Up.* American Bookseller Book of the Year Award for *The Golden Compass.*

1997 Smarties Silver Award, Rowntree Mackintosh Co., for *Clockwork, or All Wound Up.* Publishers Weekly (U.S.) Best Book of the Year for *The Subtle Knife.* Parents' Choice Gold Medal Book Award (U.S.) for *The Subtle Knife.* American Bookseller Pick of the Lists for *The Subtle Knife.* Booklist Editor's Choice (U.S.) for *The Subtle Knife.*

2000 British Book Award for best children's book for *The Amber Spyglass.*

2001 British Book Awards Author of the Year. Booker Prize long-list, 2001 for *The Amber Spyglass.* May Hill Arbuthnot Honor Lecture Award for His Dark Materials trilogy.

2002 Whitbread Children's Award, and Whitbread Book of the Year Award for *The Amber Spyglass.* Eleanor Farjeon Award for children's literature. Booksellers' Association Author of the Year Award. Shortlisted for the South Bank Show Literature Award.

2003 His Dark Materials trilogy was voted Britain's third-best-loved novel by the British public as part of the BBC's The Big Read. Spoken Word Awards, Silver award for *The Subtle Knife* box set. Pullman named a Commander of the Order of the British Empire.

2004 Spoken Word Awards–Gold award in the Children's Fiction category for BBC Cover to Cover edition of *The Tiger In The Well.*

ACHUKA–Philip Pullman, *www.achuka.co.uk/archive/interviews/ppint.php.*

Booktrusted.com–information and advice about children's, *www.book-trusted.co.uk/prizes/prizes.php4?action=2&przid=128.*

Brown, T. Interview with Philip Pullman, August 2000, *www.avnet.co.uk/amaranth/Critic/ivpullman.htm.*

Butler, Robert. *The Art of Darkness: Staging the Philip Pullman Trilogy.* London: Oberon Books, 2003.

Cornwell, John. "Some Enchanted Author," Times Online. October 24, 2004, *www.timesonline.co.uk/article/0,,2099-1311328,00.html.*

Goldthwaite, John. *The Natural History of Make-believe.* Oxford, U.K.: Oxford University Press, 1996.

Gribbin, Mary and John. *The Science of Philip Pullman's His Dark Materials.* London: Hodder Children's Books, 2003.

Guardian Unlimited Books | Review | Philip Pullman: Dreaming of spires, July 27, 2002, *http://books.guardian.co.uk/review/story/0,12084,763709,00.html.*

Jubilee Books, Author Interview–Philip Pullman, January 2004, *www.jubileebooks.co.uk/jubilee/magazine/authors/philip_pullman/interview.asp.*

Katbamna, Mira. EducationGuardian.co.uk | News crumb | Lost the plot, September 30, 2003, *http://education.guardian.co.uk/schools/story/0,5500,1052077,00.html.*

McGreevy, Ronan. *Archbishop Wants Atheist Pullman on Syllabus.* Times Online, March 9, 2004, *www.timesonline.co.uk/article/0,,1-1031866,00.html.*

The Maritime Trust, The Maritime Heritage Project: Maritime History of Gold Rush Ships, Captains, Passengers, News–Opium, *www.maritimeheritage.org/newtale/opium.html.*

Milton, John. Paradise Lost–Book 2. *www.dartmouth.edu/~milton/reading_room/pl/book_2/index.shtml.*

Pullman, Philip. "About the Author: Essays and Articles: Children's Theatre." *www.philip-pullman.com/pages/content/index.asp?PageID=106.*

———. "About the Author: I have a feeling this all belongs to me." *www.philip-pullman.com/pages/content/index.asp?PageID=84.*

————. "About the Books: Contemporary Novels: *The Broken Bridge*." *www.philip-pullman.com/pages/content/index.asp? PageID=34.*

————. "About the Worlds: Education: Isis Speech." *www.philip-pullman.com/pages/content/index.asp?PageID=66.*

————. His Dark Materials | Philip Pullman | Carnegie Medal Acceptance Speech, November 27, 1996. *www.randomhouse.com/features/pullman/philippullman/speech.html.*

————. *The Golden Compass*. New York: Knopf, 1995.

————. *Newsmakers*, Issue 2. Farmington Hills, MI: Gale Group, 2003. Reproduced in *Student Resource Center*. Detriot, MI: Gale, 2004.

————. "The Republic of Heaven." *Horn Book Magazine* (November/December 2001) Vol. 77, Issue 6, 655–668.

————. *The Ruby in the Smoke*. New York: Knopf, 1985

————. *The Subtle Knife*. New York: Knopf, 1977.

————. EducationGuardian.co.uk | eG weekly | Theatre - the true key stage, March 30, 2004. *http://education.guardian.co.uk/egweekly/story/0,5500,1180330,00.html.*

Polka Theater Web Site. About Polka Theatre. *www.polkatheatre.com/about_company.asp.*

Rabinovitch, Dina. "His Bright Materials." *Guardian UK*, December 10, 2003, *http://books.guardian.co.uk/departments/childrenandteens/story/0,60 00,1103616,00.html.*

Randall, Marta. Online Chat with Philip Pullman, February 5–9, 2001. *www.readerville.com/webx?50*

Roberts, Susan. *A Dark Agenda?* Sure Fish, November 2002. *www.surefish.co.uk/culture/features/pullman_interview.htm.*

Squires, Claire. *Philip Pullman's Dark Materials Trilogy.* New York: Continuum International Publishing Group, 2003.

Speaker Yuan, Margaret. *The London Tower Bridge*. Farmington Hills, MI: Blackbirch Press, 2004.

Townsend, John Rowe. "Paradise Reshaped." *Horn Book Magazine* (July/August 2002) Vol. 78, Issue 5, 415–421.

Tucker, Nicholas. *Darkness Visible: Inside the world of Philip Pullman.* Cambridge, U.K.: Wizard Books, 2003.

Vincent, Sally. "Driven by daemons." Guardian UK, November 10, 2001. *www.guardian.co.uk/weekend/story/0,,589797,00.html.*

Welch, Dave. "Philip Pullman Reaches the Garden." Powells.com Interviews–Philip Pullman (2000), August 31, 2000. *www.powells.com/authors/pullman.html.*

Butler, Robert. *The Art of Darkness: Staging the Philip Pullman Trilogy.* London, U.K.: Oberon Books, 2003.

Gribbin, Mary and John. *The Science of Philip Pullman's His Dark Materials.* London: Hodder Children's Books, 2003.

Tucker, Nicholas. *Darkness Visible: Inside the world of Philip Pullman.* Cambridge, U.K.: Wizard Books, 2003.

www.philip-pullman.com
> *[Philip Pullman site. This is the author's personal website. Includes biographical material, essays, interviews, and information about works-in-progress.]*

www.hisdarkmaterials.org
> *[His Dark Materials. This is one of the largest fan websites dedicated to the His Dark Materials trilogy by Philip Pullman. Contains information on various aspects of the books, movies, and its other adaptations, plus latest news on His Dark Materials trilogy and related subjects.]*

www.nationaltheatre.org.uk
> *[National Theatre. National Theatre site with a work pack about His Dark Materials. Workpack downloaded as a pdf file.]*

www.stagework.org.uk
> *[Stagework. Related information with downloadable interviews about the production of His Dark Materials trilogy at the National Theatre.]*

www.randomhouse.com/features/pullman/philippullman/index.html
> *[Philip Pullman / His Dark Materials. Random House Publishers' website on Pullman.]*

MARGARET SPEAKER YUAN is the author of two biographies: *Agnes de Mille: Dancer* (Chelsea House, 1990) and *Avi* (Chelsea House, 2005); as well as three books about world landmarks: *Royal Gorge Bridge* (Blackbirch Press, 2003), *London Tower Bridge* (Blackbirch Press, 2004), and *Arc de Triomphe* (Blackbirch Press, 2004). She is the Executive Director of the Bay Area Independent Publishers Association, a nonprofit organization that provides educational seminars on publishing in the San Francisco Bay Area. She teaches art to children with learning disabilities, and writing classes for both adults and children.